A FORCE TO BE RECKONED WITH

A FORCE TO BE RECKONED WITH

THE VIRTUE OF A PERSON'S IDENTITY

DIRE QUOTIDIAN

A FORCE TO BE RECKONED WITH
THE VIRTUE OF A PERSON'S IDENTITY

iUniverse books may be ordered through booksellers or by contacting:

iUniverse
1663 Liberty Drive
Bloomington, IN 47403
www.iuniverse.com
844-349-9409

ISBN: 978-1-5320-9599-3 (sc)
ISBN: 978-1-5320-9600-6 (e)

Library of Congress Control Number: 2020903813

Print information available on the last page.

iUniverse rev. date: 12/12/2022

CONTENTS

Introduction ix

Chapter 1 The Story 1
How Do I Celebrate My Birthday? 2
Year 1999: Ending Of A Century 4
Figure 1 5
Year 2000: Coming Of The New Century 6
Year 2001: The New Millennium 9
The Three Visions →man Arrayed In White Robe 11
Figure 2 12

Chapter 2 The Story Before The Story 13
To Understand Must Go Back To Year 1995 14

Chapter 3 Back To The Beginning 15
Year 1996: The Full Circle 15
Year 1997: Realizing My Dreams 16
1997 Haiti Vacation Time And Four Rolls Of Films 17
Haiti 20
Year 1998: The Illness 21

Chapter 4 The Catalyst 23
First Car Incident At The Job 23
Second Car Incident At The Job 24
Third Car Incident At The Job 26
Figure 3 27

Chapter 5 The Memories 29
The Premium Boat Cruise 29

Chapter 6 Freefalling ... 33
After Leaving Mitrance Corporation: Year 2000 ... 34
Millennium: Year 2001 ... 40

Chapter 7 Trading Places [Exchange Place] ... 43
First Interview ... 44
Second Interview ... 46
The Unessential Interview ... 48

Chapter 8 Rectifying The Misconception Of A Truth ... 51
Figure 4 ... 52
The Truth ... 52

Chapter 9 The Dreams And The Visions ... 53
Case Of King Solomon: The Baby Factor? ... 56

Chapter 10 The Significance Of Dreams / Visions ... 59
The Northswayn Almost Perfect Set-Up ... 60
Reverence ... 61

Chapter 11 The Nagging Feeling ... 63
The Op-Ed Article ... 65

Chapter 12 Chronological ... 67
Figure 5 ... 70

Chapter 13 That Is Why I Have Become "A Force To Reckon With" ... 71
Shellshock ... 72

Chapter 14 Character Build-Up ... 73
Staircase To Memories ... 74
The Infamous Envelop ... 76

Chapter 15 Unheed Warnings Can Lead To Adverse Result ... 79
February 2013 ... 79

Chapter 16 Dynamics At Work ... 81

Chapter 17 The Big Picture ... 83
Deliberately Targeted Car Incident ... 83
The Vortex – Tying The Mising Link ... 85

Chapter 18 With The Touch Of The Hands ... 87
The Skeptic ... 88

Chapter 19	The Accomplishments	89
Chapter 20	Thankfull	91
	Figure 6	91
	Thank You God For My Being	92
Chapter 21	The Virtue Of A Person's Identity	93
	The Answer	93
Chapter 22	Feeling Less Than A Penny	97
Chapter 23	Keeping The Faith	101
Chapter 24	Life Reward	103
	Lighted Candle	103
Chapter 25	The Scapegoat	105
Chapter 26	Total Destruction! The Day Haiti Stood Still!	111
Chapter 27	Makeshift Investigation	113
Chapter 28	The Worst And The Most Humiliating Day	115
Chapter 29	Revelation	119
	What The Fig???	119
	The Common Denominator	121
Chapter 30	Kaleidoscope	123
	Stage I - Putting The Pieces Together	124
	Stage II - Sanity Keepsake	125
Chapter 31	My Wake Up Call!	127
	Residual Effect	128
Chapter 32	Should Have Been My Full Circle?	129
	Life Matters!	129
Chapter 33	Revolution To Resolution	131
	The Virtue Of A Person's Identity	132
Chapter 34	Coming To A Full Circle	133
	Crossing The Bridge	133

INTRODUCTION

Do you believe in **GOD**? Is a question often asked to test one's faith? Being a devout catholic and a strong charismatic person, this question is as fervent to the questioner's own lack of it as it is to the responder's reply. Therefore, my suggestion is, if ever such a question is posed to you, simply say there is only one **GOD** that create all you see and not see. This is more like a safe haven, because you cannot see **HIS creation**, you are still a believer in that **GOD** is the essential of what is seen and unseen. **GOD is the believer**. Having said that, I went through tumultuous whirlwind of changes delving me into the dept of darkness beyond the **"Abyss"**, but were it not for my belief and faith, this memoir depicting **my journey to revelation** would have never been written.

Once upon a time, my life was perfect, as perfect as it can be. So private and so mine. Until one day, that all changes. Were the changes for the better? Who is to say? Because I am entwined in a Parallel Universe and a Natural Universe. Now, this is where the story of my life really gets interesting. Talking about "Life Has A Way Of Coming Back In Full Circle".

First, if you believe in the Parallel Universe, I can say for certain that it should be as easy to follow and as easy to understand. It is a story of beliefs, healings, miracles, and wholeness. The ability to see and foresee what is not readily seen by others through powers obtained by means of spiritual greatness.

Second, if you believe in the Natural Universe, then the saying that goes, "seeing is believing" also stands. I am what you would call the very existence of a phenomenon and an extraordinary "Miracle". To put it bluntly, I should not have been alive today. By all account, I should have been dead. What happened to me, is beyond my doctors' explanations and beyond anyone's comprehension to why I am still alive, but it is the will of my **GOD**, and not the will of wishful thinkers? Hence, kudos to those who do not believe in the power of **GOD**.

Now, this brings me to the caption in the "Title", that says "a force to reckon with". What does it mean to be "a force to reckon with?" It is the force of **GOD** living within you that enable you to sustain anything and at the same time the ability to make what is impossible, possible. That is why, when an outsider thinks that it can undo what **GOD** has created in true form to suit his own purpose that rest assure, it always failed for **GOD** always intervened. In other words, to have the physical body altered, and the spiritual being changed. Take for example, a doctor who does plastic surgery or reconstructive surgery, to change someone's appearance or rather a preacher who preach about God to change one's spiritual inclination. But my situation is much more complicated than that and much more unbelievable. That is why, my life came back to me in full circle. To go from existence to nonexistence and back to existence is by **GOD'S** true nature and will. One cannot erase what **GOD** has created, nor can one reign supreme in **GOD'S** kingdom.

My Catholic upbringing made me superior in my **GOD'S** faith. My continuous catholic religion keeps me in touch with **GOD'S** truths and ways.

CHAPTER I
THE STORY

The Story Begins. Let me start with the former! The Parallel Universe is an intricate phenomenon where one seems to be existing in two places at once. Now I didn't know this was ever possible nor quite understand that this kind of phenomenon does happen therefore, I could not name it. It wasn't until when I had picked up a book to read of **PADRE PIO**, that I found the word for it. What I had experienced is called "BILOCATION"? What is a Bilocation? Quoting from the famous book of Padre Pio, **"A bilocation is a miraculous phenomenon of being in two different places at the same time. In one place the person is present in body; while in the other, he is there in spirit clothed with what appears to be his physical body."**

(***Padre Pio – The Wonder Worker, by Bro. Francis Mary Kalvelage, F.I., Editor (List 12.50) 1999***)

[Now do not be fooled by others claiming to know the true stories, as they do not know for their versions are just that, made-up versions or make-believes.]

I Am So Happy. Notice that I started the text with I am so happy. I deliberately did this to prepare you for what to come of the many journeys and passages in my life. How one moment, you can be in a state of exuberant and the next you are free falling into an endless abyss? I do not know when it all started, but I do know the sequences from the beginning to the present. What to come of the future is fascinating? I know for I was the past, now the present, and hopefully the future. But most important, is how I came back full circle and learned to celebrate my birthday again?

HOW DO I CELEBRATE MY BIRTHDAY?

How Do I Celebrate My Birthday?

When it is a constant reminder of 9/11?
I know I should count all my Blessings,
But it is so hard to do when it is only two days before and after.
The memories lingered on and on with each new passing day.
No, I shall never forget those who died.
May GOD look upon their families and ease their burden.

***How Do I Celebrate My Birthday?
For Birthdays come and go,
But they always come back.
It is life refresh, rejuvenate and renew.
It is a way of saying you are ALIVE!***

The things I used to do and love
Are now memories of the person I once were?
I have to learn to move on, get passed it and,
Do not let that date define who I become.
Somehow, I know the answer is in me.
Only I can bring myself out of this melancholy.

***How Do I Celebrate My Birthday?
For Birthdays come and go,
But they always come back.
It is life refresh, rejuvenate and renew.
It is a way of saying you are ALIVE!***

The month of September used to bring me Joy!
And how I relished in its coming?

Labor Day, back to school; Fall, change of the season;
Life, my Birthday.
But now 9/11, that took so many lives
Brought forth devastating Memories
That no one can change it for me but me.

***How Do I Celebrate My Birthday?
For Birthdays come and go,
But they always come back.
It is life refresh, rejuvenate and renew.
It is a way of saying you are ALIVE!***

I know I must be strong.
But when reality sets in and the memories come back,
I cannot hide the fact that it hurts so bad.
It has been said that time would heal all wounds,
But why is my heart at a standstill.
When Birthdays are reminder of one Existence?

***How Do I Celebrate My Birthday?
For Birthdays come and go,
But they always come back.

It is life refresh, rejuvenate and renew.
It is a way of saying you are ALIVE!***

Lately, I find it hard to hold on,
When my world is in a whirlwind?
No, I will not let evil destroy what is good.
But let us give credence to Life!
I never was one to make such a big deal of Birthdays
Until I have learned the value of Life.
That Life is GOD'S way of saying you survived.

*****Happy Birthday To Me!**
Happy Birthday To September!
Happy Birthday to LIFE!***

YEAR 1999: ENDING OF A CENTURY

The year which marked the beginning of events to follow. Little did I know then that the year would be an eventful one, with many twists and turns. So many mistakes and errors were made mostly due to blindsight. This was supposed to be the year where I would make all my dreams come true for me. Those unfinished ideas and creations that I had started in the past I was going to make it happen with the coming new Century. I went right into the creative mode, the learning mode, and the business mode. I thought I was set, ready and go to tackle once again my **Convertipants, the Convertible Jeans** and turn it into reality. But in hindsight, circumstances happened! I now see what I could not see then, why at that time, when I first introduced my creation to ISO things moved at a very slow pace. Come to find out, I never did receive the portion of the statement that requested for a personal photo/portrait of the creator to attach to one's project in order to prevent anyone from becoming the unanimous inventor and hijacked the real creator's project. After all the trips I made, going to and from the many interviews, starting with the Central City Office where the contract originated and then The Centre Office. I can't help but to wonder if it were not a race issue or maybe an accent issue. Either way, crazy stuffs started to happen. In all honesty, I regretted things turned out the way it did, for I do admit, ISO did an excellent job upon my requests. The artwork was beautiful, the caption was captivating, and the description was amazing. All the hard work never was completed as my life almost ended. As a result, one then cannot help but becoming cynical and wondering was the planning to hijacked one's creation started from the beginning or later in time the idea just manifested itself. Regardless, by the grace of **GOD**, what one hopes to happen did not happen.

The Almost Perfect Set-Up At STARLIGHT: Someone from my past started hanging around with me. Little did I know it then that what had seemed to be innocent hangouts with an old acquaintance would turn out to be many uneventful schemes of tragedies happening to me that would have dire consequences later in my life. The person would come and picked me up to go to Starlight, in Central City. The nights-out to the club continued for awhile until early 1999 when the last time I was taken there to Starlight that the person revealed to me and showed me while driving to Central City her big Diamond Ring. About some hours later from the Starlight club, we went to another club in Hunztown at Cokou's by the water. (Connecting the dots: soon afterwards, a spur of Cokou's chains stores/boutiques sprung up all over in County Banque.) Unbeknownst to me, that I would have a target on my back, when by July 1999 my new car was side-swiped by an unstable person named "Jane Doe" on a Sunday Afternoon at Jamestown Avenue in County Banque. This whole mess of incident with my car always troubled me and felt like a target. Also, totally escaped my mind was that such person was trying to reach her boyfriend cop with a cellular phone when such instrument was unheard of back then to the mass population.

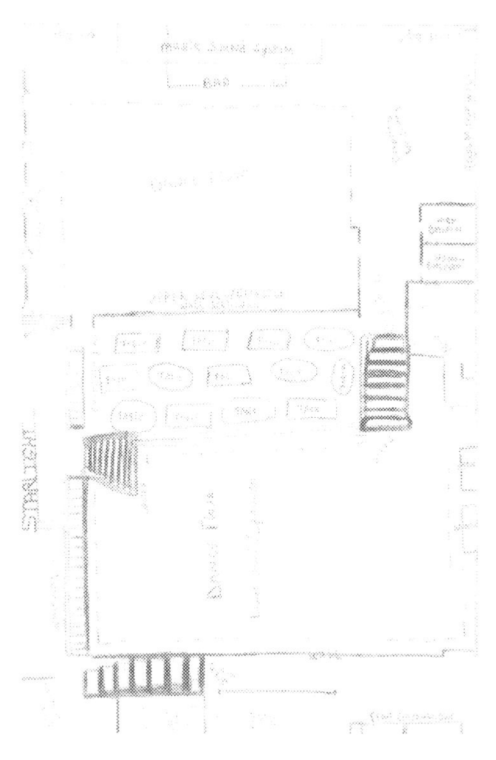

Figure 1

Nineteen hundred ninety-nine, didn't exactly started out bad but it sure got worse. Now back to reality! Upbeat and go lucky through it all without even realizing how serious was my illness. I have a knack for making things look a lot easier than it actually is. Maybe that would explain why at that time, noone close to me knew how serious and gravely ill I was. That is why I will always sing GOD's praises and forever be thankful. One thing for sure about the saying that goes something like this, "innocent is bliss" is for the naïve. Life is in a constant motion; one cannot stand by and watch things happen for Life does not stop for no one. The stages that we all go through are set in intervals with time either a friend or a foe. What one puts in is what one gets out? Input is always equal to Output, except for the fact that only few individuals have surpassed life's expectations. Thus, I was very excited. I took a cruise trip just to get out of the mundane routine and cleared my mind. Relaxed for awhile! Who knew that the trip would have had its consequences? Maybe that was when my passport information was taken for mischievous purposes thus resulting in Identity Theft.

YEAR 2000: COMING OF THE NEW CENTURY

I spent two months at Mitrance Corporation when it got too much to bear that I shed some tears. Could it have been a premonition of what to come? Right there and then in that kitchen/office a vision came before me and it was dreadful. I can't remember or don't know if it was something I saw or someone I saw. I started not feeling well around March 2000 so much so that I had to leave the Mitrance Corporation job in May 2000. Was it then the beginning of my demise from whatever was reeking havocs in my system?

Don't Cry Me A River Of Tears.
Don't Cry Me An Ocean Of Sorrows.
Don't Cry Me A Sea Of Reasons.
I Don't Need Excuses,
Just Give Me The Facts.

Then before I knew it, the year 2000 is at the end and we about to welcome the new year 2001. Feeling like I have been out of commission for the whole year and having been unproductive, I could not let the year go by without partaking in it. So, I decided on New Year's Eve, December 31st, 2000 to go to Times Square in "The City" and celebrate with the crowd in welcoming the new year as I have seen on the television. (I have never done this before, first time at a major crowd gathering; needed to think and clear my head.) Earlier that day, the plan was for my sister and I to go together in "The City" for the celebration but as the day wined down and it was time to leave, my sister changed her mind and decided not to go afterall. Therefore, I had to borrow $20 dollars from her to make the traveling to New York by myself for the festive. I boarded the bus from home and went to the subway and took the train to "The City". When I got there, it was eight o'clock pm (that was about four hours from the countdown waiting in the cold).

First thing I did coming out of the subway was to buy a cup of chocolate at the coffee stand in order to keep myself warm. There were a lot of blockages starting at the Main Entrance Station that continued on every block as one would exit out of the subway and coming upon officers ushering us back in the opposite direction from whence, we first got off the train stop. As it turned out, each block was the same reappearing occurrences over and over again that I had to walk back many blocks to finally end up on the back-end of the street blockage where there was finally a clearance and the officers were letting people in to stand. (Had I known this would have been the case, I would have gotten off at that particular Subway Stop beforehand because I ended-up there anyway?)

<u>There Were Two Divided Sectors:</u>

I finally ended up in the front of the **Second Sector** where the police barricades formed and waited and waited as the sector started filling with new commers. At the same time and with each passing minute, the temperature started to drop and drop and drop until it got into the single digit and later below zero degree. I could not feel my toes, my feet and my legs as I stood there waiting some more. Something unnerving happened and I saw something but what? I cannot remember it now, but it happened close to the sidewalk; where there was a restaurant named after a famous star and a commotion was going on but what? Don't remember? Most of the police officers seemed to congregate around that vicinity and they were talking among themselves. (I heard something but what? I cannot remember it now.)

It was a very long night; waited on hours after hours and hours. As the hours wore off, the temperature kept dropping and with each new hour, it got colder, so cold, it became unbearable and uncomfortable and the crowd behind me got very unruly as younger and younger males found their way behind me and using fouled languages (might be group of college students). At some point, it got so tight that they were pressing against me and relieving themselves right there in front of people that I went off on them and told them what they were? I could not take it anymore and so I asked one officer close to the sidewalk if I could be moved to a lesser crowded spot at the end of the **First Sector** where there was clearly empty space and he obliged.

The officer moved the barricade and allowed me to get out and walked to the end of the back of the line in the **First Sector**. What a relief it was for me? If I had stayed there any longer and a minute more, I think I would have passed out or go into panic attack? And so, I went to the **First Sector** where it was less crowded and more room to breathe when, all of a sudden, out of nowhere this very tall man came and stood next to me and we started talking (nothing much, just about the weather and the New Year's Festive). More times have passed and then many officers on horses came out and lined in formation in front of the restaurant. If it were not for the tall man by my side, who pointed out to me the activity, I would have missed it? They were displaying their techniques on horses (it was impressive); and then they divided into groups, and some left and crossed to the other side of the street. Afterward, maybe about forty-five minutes later, the big moment came, the count down to the New Year and that was that! Wow!!! I froze my butt for nothing, so I told myself right then and there never to do this again because it is much better on Television. All the hoopla was for nothing! All I got out of it was jerks pressing against me; freezing my whole body to the bones; and in addition to the distance from the ball dropping I could not see anything. In any event, I set out and did what I said I was going to do. I am a person of my words. That is why I do not talk much? If I said I am going to do something, I do it! **My Motto is, less Talk and more Action!**

Even as I am writing this account of events, something crossed my mind that this very tall man may have been my angel in disguised, for he stayed with me 'till the end of the night and even offered to walk the distance with me back to the subway to catch the train back home. Mind you, I did not come with this man, but he came to the line that I was in the "City" and now he is escorting me back home. I paid my fair and went through the turnstile and boarded the train, he too was there by my side. We sat side by side in the two seaters inside the train, I, by the window seat and he, by the aisle seat. And just like that, as he came out of nowhere and stood by me in the "City", he disappeared just like that when we came to the end of our journey at the last stop on the train route to Eastside Place.

(**May GOD bless him, whoever you were?**)

YEAR 2001: THE NEW MILLENNIUM

This year marked the year of my encountered with the phenomenon of the "bilocation". Between the hours of 7am to 8pm, everything was going well as I boarded the transit bus to my destination in Triomphe Place. The route of the bus normally goes smoothly and quickly but on that particular day, the traffic got hectic and the bus moved at a very slow speed to almost a stop. Then something unusual happened, as it got close to its final stop, it made a detour and came to its destination at the Quelche Mall. By that time, it started to rain lightly and I was running out of time but instead of walking the extra distance to the Examination Building on Maynard Boulevard, I decided to go down the subway and boarded the train to that one stop to the Shuttle Drive and got off. Upon, emerging from the subway into the openness of the street above, I opened the umbrella and stepped onto the sidewalk going eastbound. Since I got out on the wrongside of the street instead of where I should have exited on the westbound, I had to cross that big intersection to get to the right side on the other side. Hence, I looked both ways from right to left, when this (vision) happened? *Looking back now, could this have been a premonition of being at a crossroad? I saw this man clothed in all-white from head to toe stooped down in a sitting position on the sidewalk with a dog by his side. Now thinking back, it was strange that the man's clothing did not appear to get wet, dirty, nor messy with mud since it was raining and coming down heavy as he had no umbrella and no cover while he was out in the open. Instead, the clothing remained completely white as snow. I was so focused on getting to the test-site that it did not occur to me that things seemed out of place. The streets were cleared, and I proceeded to cross that huge intersection to the westbound side. I got to the building and went inside to the testing office, put my stuff in the locker and waited to be called upon for ID verification. When it was my turn, the black woman, administering the test-site said she could not let me in the test-room because I entered the office after 8am and that was considered late to process me, although the regular scheduled exam does not start until 8:30am. I pleaded with her to let me take the test since it was not even 8:30am yet but only 8:15am and she finally checked me in. The "Exam" was a two-hour test that was programed in advance. She directed me to the first computer within the sectional against the wall then registered me on the computer to begin taking the test. I sat down and quickly started with the "Exam". Sometimes within fifteen (15) minutes of the test my computer just frozen. Then the black woman reappeared into the test-room and told me that she made a mistake with positioning me on this computer and moved me to another computer in the inner sectional aisle. Once again, I had to restart the exam, but I was reassured that all the questions I had previously answered within the fifteen (15) minutes would not be affected but would be transferred over and I would not miss a thing. At that time, I was not bother by the interruption because I was very confident and knew the materials well. But little did I know then, there were too many red flags that should have warranted for my concerns.

What was especially strange, was the fact that the guy beside me was covered from head to toe in turbine and seemed very edgy? (Made the hairs stood up on my arms). All this would lead into the revelation that the computer-switch, the data manipulation, the reversal of number 3 into the letter "E" and the Identity Theft compounded to what would lead up to that Unfateful Day Of Collateral Damage on September 11, 2001.

THE THREE VISIONS →MAN ARRAYED IN WHITE ROBE

1. **What is the revelation? Why appear to me?**
2. **3X you appeared→Fourth (4th) Never happened→Fifth (5th) Vision Is The Missing Link**
3. **Why do you keep reoccurring in my Dreams?**
4. **My revelation is the tell-tale of a warning.**

I am getting closer to know who you are? The "LAMB" that will receive all his glories when the switch-a-woo shall be switched back to the original state. Beware of the subject that took on the appearance of the "LAMB" will lose her identity forever. Whenever one appeared, the other one is never around? Two women stepped into one man's shoes and for that to have happened, would require a lot of accomplices (not only CHRIST had to face one/Judas, but also had to face Pontius Pilate surrounded by traders).

True to its form, a "vision" is a chance occurrence with its own timing. Noone can predict when in a lifetime, one is going to encounter the Splendor Of Magnificence and how one reacts to it? I would like to think that even in my blissful ignorance that the course of action that I had made in that moment was the right one. Timing is everything and it halts for no man, action, event, nor disaster. In my mind's eyes, I did not think to make much of anything with the "vision" I saw except that I had an "Exam" to take. I never saw a face except that he was arrayed in White-Light and had a Majestic Aura about him. That is why I remembered until now the "vision"? I wished I could have gone back in time and walked toward the "vision" instead of going to the office but wishing and hoping would not have changed the occurrences on that day for it is human nature to do what one predestined or planned to do. Even if I were to be enlightened on that day, still I woke up with one track mind and that was the "Exam". Mishap or not, I do believe that the "vison" appeared for a reason and it is a reason that I shall never know for I missed my opportunity when I crossed the street to the other side and turned it into a crossroad.

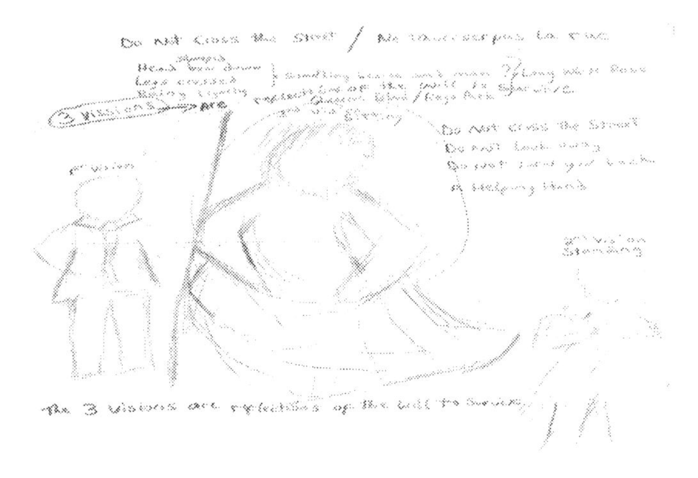

Figure 2

Dated: October 7, 2007

But I have seen such a face again during my work-life. Where? I cannot remember.

My first encountered was at Quelchetown College Library. I did not have a clue that such a person was present for I always have my head down and buried in my books studying. But I did notice someone was looking at me and as I lifted my head, the person lowered his. Then he came over and handed me a piece of paper (his drawings – by Master Luminate).

CHAPTER II

THE STORY BEFORE THE STORY

The Story Continues. The latter is even better. The Natural Universe is the realm of reality, of actuality, and of practicality. Logic tells us that, what is tangible can be touched, what is audible can be heard, and what is sightly can be seen. How can then this not be so wonderful? To be a part of a world where one can exist in a universe that is in its natural state.

You have heard about **DOUBLE INDEMNITY**, well it happened to me but not in the way I would have liked it to happen nor not like the movies. Mine was more on the sinister side. It was as if, someone was trying to replace me. Remember this Date: January 29, 2002 at 2:25:37PM, the day and time my floppy disc was duplicated and erased at the Quelche Borough Public Library in Central City. My beautiful writings, poems and lyrics were stolen and being used in the most vile and despicable ways as if **concocted** into a life of its own.

I became the "scapegoat"! The Almost Perfect Set-Up. Fighting to keep my sanity. Making me looked like the insane one. The Dire Quotidian that almost non-existed. That is why "Life has a way of coming back in full circle"?

All this would be better explained in later chapters and in its entirety but for now, let us stay on track and continued with this chapter. To scapegoat an innocent person and discredit that person's reputation is a flaw in the instigator's own make-up of his/her humanity that makes him/her incapable of wanting to destroy someone else's self-esteem. Your character is your very essence of who you are and what you are? Sometimes in life, you must become a character in order to combat whatever negativities encountered so as not to fall prey to victimization. It does not mean to be overtly arrogant or obnoxious. (Instead humble oneself and become meek and humble like **JESUS** is Victorious.)

TO UNDERSTAND MUST GO BACK TO YEAR 1995

THE AWARENESS: Put Ideas Into Motion.

The year that I became a full pledge citizen of the good old United States of America. I started putting my plans into motion and looking forward to the future. I can visualize my dreams taking form. I did everything right by sending out my work and revisiting my "Jeans Invention". Already, I can feel success within reach and my hands reaching for the American Dream and holding on real tight.

(Back then, I should have been more aware and keener to the fact that someone was indeed following me. But I brushed it off as just my nerves and being overly sensitive. Surprised, surprised, to my chagrin my intuition proved to be right, much, much, much later in my life and almost to my demise.)

Magnificent at work, the creation of the **Convertipants @ La Dire** originated in 1988 that would copulate the Pants Industry as it revolutionized the Jeans World by embodies fashion, style, wearable, and accessibility into one package. It was during my college years in 1988 that I had the concept for the Jeans. Come to find out, years later that this was a significant year in the church world, for it marked "The Year That Is The End Of The Church Year". The "JEANS" that changes with the season. It has many functions and purposes for instance, by unzipping a portion of the pants leg would accommodate a broken leg in a cast. Interest for it would be worldwide as beneficial to all age groups. Outlook and promises are that it would evolve with time and would deliver as it says, "seeing is believing".

CHAPTER III
BACK TO THE BEGINNING

How Interesting That "Life Has A Way Of Coming Back In Full Circle"? No matter how one tries to direct one life or tries to make it into something other than, if **GOD** is not willing, who is to say where life will lead you? A famous proverb that my fellow Christians go by "L'homme propose mais DIEU dispose." This will keep you forever grounded and in the right path of righteousness.

YEAR 1996: THE FULL CIRCLE

The line that saved me from going to the end and right back to the beginning, was when I made the choice to accept GOD as the Believer? I have the gift of GOD in me.

The year should have been my year of success. I have already published my writings and won the "Diamond Homer Trophy" award, of which I never received.

But, as life would have it, for some strange reason, I was let go from the job with Tigwa Co. on Maynard Boulevard in County Banque. At first, I was upset because it was a setback and I had to move out of the Triomphe Place Apartment which I loved so much. Then by the end of August I have found a new job with Forthway Right, Inc. Had I known that within a month I would have started a new job I would have stayed in the Apartment? I enjoyed being on my own, my independence and loved the location near by the Quelche Mall. One thing I have learned from this experience, is that never questioned "the hands of time" for years later, it would be proven to me that was an actual **"Blessing In Disguise"**. Sometimes things do happen for a reason, **GOD'S angels were looking out for me.**

I should have let by-gone be by-gone but I was so ticked off at the way I got escorted out the building like a common "nobody". I had put in my sweat and hardwork into that job for one year and one month and even did extra time when requested, on calls when needed and just like that, with no explanation I was booted out. And so, I did what a logical person would do in an unjust situation, I filed a legal suit. BIG MISTAKE! Did not know it then that it would carry over to my new job? Boy-oh-Boy! What a dumb idea it was then? But it was too late, what was done was done? I really did not know it then that it would have taken me a month to get another job for in the past it normally took me two months to six months of a gap to get to the next job.

When I finally started my new job with Forthway Right, Inc., it was great and elated for me because I was literally starting from scratch and helping to build the office into shape. What a concept that was? I was involved in the building process of a new office. It started with two people in the Administrative Team and then later the office became fully staffed. Well, that did not last for long. In hindsight, I can see now why it was "ICY" with me? I had that lingering lawsuit hanging over my head. As Murphy Laws would say: "What would go wrong would go wrong?" Indeed, it did! It never fails! And it could not have come at the worst time, when a year later I was awarded the company stock certificate for a job well done and for my hardwork and effort. (A beautiful appreciation and recognition for work well done.)

YEAR 1997: REALIZING MY DREAMS

This year was the happiest year of my life. Finally, I saw the opportunity to make my dreams come true. I had everything organized and planned. I was finally ready to put to work my project: **Convertible Jeans @ Dire Quotidian or Dire Inc.** I wanted to revolutionize the Pants World.

Strangely enough, I did something that I would normally not do, I went and took commercial classes to get the feel of marketing oneself (meaning, I put myself out there.) I took many courses in the field of insurance to familiarize myself with the industry.

To start with, when the opportunity presented itself, I made the trip to my homeland where I was born. Do some research of my birthplace and analyze the essentials of incorporating fashion. I wanted to bring some incentives to the Country. Perhaps, more like a boost to the economy and to get it started. Why not give something back to HAITI? It was well thought out idea that got detour because of the mishap with the house.

Vacation Preparation: Brought camera, four (4) rolls of films…Before going and one week prior to the vacation, I had braided my own hair (had extension braids in my hair). Thus, when I went back to work in the office with the braids in my hair to finish that one week before leave of absent. The Disparity. Two weeks of Vacation Time and off to the Airport from NY to Haiti that would take approximately three (3) hours. Upon arrival in Haiti, I got picked up from the Airport to House on Rue Elle Alette, in Port-Au-Prince. Many sightseeing, adventures, walks and sceneries. While there, I went to one wedding event, late at night, midnight, rainy day. Did not get to see the couples? On the final day; back to the U.S.A. I took the braids out and came back to work without them and as me before.

1997 HAITI VACATION TIME AND FOUR ROLLS OF FILMS

For so long, the Virgin Mary was speaking to me and I could not understand. She appeared to me in my dreams and made a declaration that specifically signified "The Rose".

Back in 1997, when I went to Haiti, I took along my camera and took numerous pictures (recording a documentary). Somehow, when I got back to the U.S., and brought those four films to be developed at the Squarespace Photo Shop, in Quelchetown, my pictures just disappeared. (Now this is the same place where I have been doing business with for many years, all my past pictures got developed there). A fool at the place told me that everything registered blanks and there was nothing on those films. Imaging my astonishment, is an understatement. In any event, what started way back, is now about to come to a completion, as I am the completer. Those four films do exist.

Out of all the sceneries of lies being played according to my documentary on those four films, one is being kept out. The right one, is the school that I went to as a child. The school that thought us from earlier on that GOD is the way. All the props are being given to the brotherhoods of the priestly congregation what about the sisterhoods of the convent, who formed the minds of the young little sisters like me. It was by far, through their education that shaped my mind into being the valor student. It was not a brother who first perceived the notion of making a documentary but a sister that set out on her own to do just that. Hence, a fellow countryman has taken my documentary under false pretense and then presenting it as facts without even knowing the full story or having had firsthand knowledge. No wonder the **Rosa Mystica** (one of the many 42 facets of the **Virgin Mary**) was beside herself and kept appearing to me in my dreams. Something was just not right. How conniving that brother must be to stoop this low? Did not the parochial school teach them the morals of good conduct? To have this great dimension of knowledge is greatly supported by the fact that the parochial school of sisterhood outperformed and outsmarted the brotherhood school since the basic element of moral conduct is to tell the truth always.

I always felt from the beginning that, it must have been someone who knew of my every moves and actions, even down to the book that I was reading. Why would a peaceful country such as Haiti, now imploring the ideology of kidnapping, a term they never heard of or even contrive in their minds? All that ugliness and vagabonds being transported to this beautiful, once upon a time a paradise of a country. This mean-spirited fellow-countryman was truly ugly in all forms as GREED was the main underlying motive.

The **Virgin Mary** is calling to me time after time to correct this ill-fated and misguided abomination. Why would an upright country of good standards, is now turned upside-down and inside-out where the laws do not apply? How in heavens' name, did that vagabonds have an upper hand in the functional of a country, through MANIPULATION?

The Parochial School of Sisters.
Highly the Academic of Spiritual Excellence.
Highly the Educator of Intelligence.
Highly the Magnificence of Brilliance.
Highly the Motivator of Individuality.
Highly the Transformer of Wisdom.

"We truly believed in the instruments of Peace, Love, Pardon, Faith, Hope, Light and Joy." We were the epitome of the Proper Little Ladies of Mercy.

I started writing prayers at a very young age through the instructions of the sisters at the school. As an adult, my prayers have evolved and became more profound. Now I get it, why my first real prayer "Thank You God For My Being" was about. At that time, I did not know it then, but I was searching for that form of spiritual guidance that was lacking in my life. The real essence of being a child of GOD.

This brings me back to the real issue at hand, the fact that, an insidious man stole my identity. The very notion of it, sicken me. How polite that I am being in calling this vagabond, insidious when he has taken what is good, made it fouled, and making a mockery of everything? As greedy as he may have been, but there is a limit. This limit is called the reckoning of days to come when he shall be subject to the criminal justice system. Now if this jerk of a man has had an ounce of intelligence maybe it would not have been so bad, but the man is a total buffoon. Cannot cut it in the real world, had to steal a woman's Identity. Mind you, a woman of wordily intelligence (hence, the stalking must have started from the beginning, the contemplation). How does one accomplish this feast might have been through the world of technology...the data manipulation... where peoples' information lingers in cyberspace? This might explain the massive blackout with all the computers and the reorganization of Data. Binary numbers are inputs of "1" and "0" one does not necessarily need a high IQ to work with just two numbers that required only manual functions and no thought process.

Getting back my good name was only the beginning. There are still more matters that need to be rectified, "The Purification Of The Most Blessed Virgin Mother".

HAITI

When I went to the school and took those pictures, there was an unusual guy lurking about? Since I keep hearing the phrase, "Mélange", could it possibly be that the sisters have encountered problems due to compromising position brought on them as the result of those stolen pictures?

THE ROSE GARDEN: Sometimes in life, people fabricate lies to undermine a correctly functional system. The School is an excellent school of academic performance. Now I believe for false lies to take hold and have some merit of truth to it, one must look at the possibility that it was an inside job. It is like there are two sides to a story and the truth. Now the truth is the real story. JESUS is the truth and the way. All the young children were properly taken care of with the emphasis on education. To find the truth it is imperative to look at both sides, if a grievous party had some issues way back then and now decided to take this opportunity to blasphemies the good name of the school, then look at all the relevant and pertinent facts. What is the academic report of this individual, what kind of student was that individual and last, but not least the individual status? I remembered a story which I came to believe was not true but made up because someone was angry. The Story was about some few students messing and roughing the sisters' Rose Gardens. They were caught and were reprimanded. Yes, the sisters had every right to punish the students in question. I strongly believe in that. But the students had no right to fabricate the lies that they told afterward. Now the lies told, were that the students were roughly treated and were put in a dark closed space supposedly filled with "snakes", turned out to be untrue. Firstly, the school is a school of educators, not a place where one keeps animals. Secondly, why is that those are the only few students this happened to when the school has been functioning for the longest times without any prior incidents. Thirdly, as I can remembered clearly, there was not a buzz about this lie the day it occurred or the next day and not even the year as we were all prelude to daily information. And fourthly, would not the parents of said students have made a big stink about the incident at that time when it occurred and if, only if it really happened?

Sometimes kids have a way of making things up and getting grown-ups in trouble just to get their ways. Usually and at most, it is the unruly children that are hard to discipline that have the wildest imaginations and created things that can undermine the true situation. Do not take for granted the cunningness at which they can depict one grown-up against another. I wonder if that girl who started and made up this lie had good grades while in the school, perhaps, "NO". I can say for sure that I know without a doubt, that the girl did not have an excellent academy.

In summation, the truth shall be told. The day that lies become "the truth" is the day that abomination takes precedence. Since when do illiterates have the wisdom and the knowledge to Function without rules and regulations. Maybe the process for reconciliation can be and should be resolved? The service is render and the truth inscribe. It is time to get back the true beauty of our **Lady Of The Rose: Rosa Mystica, the lady of truth.**

YEAR 1998: THE ILLNESS

So Much Have Happened In This Year Alone. Dealing with my father's death in May and then battling with the house mishap.

AND THEN IT BEGAN: THE FLU SHOT Dated: October 16, 1998

Because I started the month with a minor cold that grew into a persistent harsh coughing, I went to get my flu shot/vaccination in Quelchetown. Why??? I can't remember the exact details nor recall what particularly prompted me to go visit his office for my flu shot but I did go for the following reasons: 1) Suffering from a severe and terrible flu that developed into this bad, scratchy and nonstop coughs. 2) Attending classes and preparing to take the next "Exam2" with three weeks into the course, I could not miss anymore sessions as classes do not repeat. Last but, not least 3) I had to do something about the cough / hence the vaccination but instead it got worst after the shot. Therefore, I followed someone advice and went to get the flu shot. What happened after the vaccination was unimaginable?

There must have been an angel by my side. Truly in our lives, we all need a good angel at one point or another. The angel that protects, prevents and guides us according to GOD's will. The big break that I have been waiting for, just fell right into my lap. An amazing gift was bestowed upon me that afforded me the incentives to move forward and get started with my dreams again. Finally, I can be established. That's when it all started, that terrible flu. It seemed like an endless fever that refused to go away. No matter what I did, do and took, the fever persisted and would not disappear. Thus, someone suggested that I should go and see the doctor for the flu, I did just that. Instead of getting better, I got worst. Maybe it was an allergic reaction to the vaccination.

On that day, I took a sick day from work and went to my 1pm appointment - it was just a quick shot that took 3 seconds. Now the pondering question is "How did I know of this place and why did I go there?" Needless, to say, the doctor saw me and gave me the vaccine on my left upper arm. Noteworthy to mention, the office was close by the Town's College and maybe as a former student of the Town's College, we might have taken our flushot there. Following that week on October 19, 1998, I became very dehydrated and loss a lot of weight (to be exact, I was Pencil Thin). In addition to that, I also had severe diarrhea.

CHAPTER IV
THE CATALYST

Acts And Causes Of A Chain Reaction. The Domino Effect.

FIRST CAR INCIDENT AT THE JOB:

On Friday, July 23, 1999 between the hours of 1pm and 2pm, the "Vehicle Endangerment" took placed due to intent of maliciousness and mischievousness. Imagine what would have happen had I gotten into a car accident with two small children inside the car-----Unforgiveable? Sweet Honey Ice Tea!!! Someone stuck a big nail into the back of my left car tire.

Mental and Physical Distress-----kept thinking and visualizing all the possibilities of **"What-Ifs?"** with the two children in the car with me and in harms' way. This still weighted heavily on my mind.

On Friday after worktime – and around 12pm, Karmar brought the children inside the office as I had requested him to for a visit with the co-workers. Since I had their pictures on my desk, they were asking me when they were ever going to meet the children and since on Fridays, the company let out early I figured I would surprise them by bringing the children in. Well it did not turn out the way I expected instead in hindsight, it was just the beginning of my nightmares to come at the office. After my brother brought in the two children, he stepped out of the building and I was in the office with the two small children, the baby in my arms at all time and the 8-year old got separated from me and went off with the other workers and into the manager's office with supervisor, assistant and representative. What they talked about? I would not know because I had no preview to it. Now to think of it and looking back, I think they were trying to distract me and keep me away from him. I guessed they wanted alone time with him. Why??? 'Till this day, it is anybody guess. Only the 8-year old could say what went on back then, only if he could remember. As for me, I remained stationed in the kitchen with the baby in my arms while the two men were talking and inquiring about the children. At one point, one of the men tried to elicit a reaction from the baby got nothing but blank stared. And then I tapped on her arm, liked padded it and still got no reaction. She did not even cry nor blink her eye. And when it was time for me to leave, I packed up and went into my car in the parking lot where I met with my brother and he helped me put the children into the car. Where the 8-year old sat in the passenger seat and the baby my brother placed in her carseat that was on the backseat behind the driverside. Afterwards, I got into the driverseat and drove the car home and it was not until I got home and getting out of the car that I noticed that "there was a screw in the backrear tire" where the baby was in her carseat. **"A lot of What-Ifs"???** How could anyone create a vehicle endangerment while children were in the car? Sometime after the incident, which weighted heavily on me, the endangerment of children, I became distraught for every time I would see a baby, I would have flashback memories of **"What-Ifs?"** What always troubled me about that screw in the back tire was that, I did not hear a blast or a pop if I had run over it on the road? Because I had the baby in the car and she was sleeping in the backseat, I did not play the radio. Therefore, I should have heard something if I had run over it. But that was not the case! Instead, the tire remained intact with no flat except for that screw inserted inside the tire.

SECOND CAR INCIDENT AT THE JOB:

On August 2, 1999-----As always, on my lunch hour, I got in my car and drove out of the parking lot to go out to eat off the premises. Upon my returned from lunch and back into the parking lot, as I pulled into the same spot that I was in before and parked the car, I then proceed to come out of the car and as I opened the driverside door and stepped out unto the lot and **"Boom"** it hit me. The squashed mouse by my car during lunch break started me on a spinned-off. Boy-oh-boy! That almost gave me a heart attack. I could not stop screaming and went into shocked. How I got out of it and snapped back is a wonder still? Somehow or another, I managed to compose myself and went back inside the building and to work at my desk trying hard not to show any signs of my previous frenzy. But I could not stop shaking and I had to do something to get it out of my system and hence, I composed that infamous **"Harassment Email"** to home office legal counselor explaining that I need to report an incident but did not go into any specific details which must have sent them into a tailspin. Neither was I thinking straight, for whenever "harassment" is mentioned in an office, it is always assumed that it involved a male person (generalization). It was not until I got home and cooled off that I realized I had made a mistake in composing that email and when the following next day came, and I got back in the office, first thing I did was quickly typed a recant email to the legal counselor and informed him that I no longer want to pursue the matter. Still without explicit explanation to what perspired, I had left the door open to "misinterpretations". When all this had to do is with a **squashed/smashed rat** by my car in the parking lot that almost rendered me a heart attack? I had to vent out my frustration because there was no way I had accepted a job to be in a kiddy show or a school play of teenagers reliving their yesteryears. I thought we were mature adults here making a living. We all had responsibilities to get up in the morning to come to work and make an honest living. And so, I thought, and it became the beginning of my downfall; letting my guard down!

◆◆◆

On top of that, a lot of mischievous things were going on around my desk. I would find the heads of my statues broken on my desk. One day, after coming from lunch and finding unusual items around my cubicle, I got so enraged with annoyance that I walked down the cubicle aisle and ram-up my arm against it and banged my wrist pretty bad. I thought I had broken my arm that day. Then Thursday, August 26, 1999 came around and I had to go get my right arm checked due to the swelling of the wrist and paid a co-pay of $15 at the Squarespace Radiology in County Banque. First time I ever did anything drastic as to go get prescription (VIOXX) from a doctor for the swollen to come down along for the pain to subside.

THIRD CAR INCIDENT AT THE JOB:

By September 24, 1999, my life changed forever, it was a Friday afternoon when the office let out early (12pm) that I set off and went to my scheduled appointment with Doctor Milvern in the Knoorblart Clinic Office. I should have taken it as a sign when all the forces where working against me finding the place but being the stubborn that I am, never mind that I was getting lost, going around in circles, and still getting lost time and time again, and because it was still early in the afternoon, I kept on going until I finally find the red brick building by mistake after making one good turn. I got there late and missed my timeslot and the young man behind the desk counter told me I had to wait. Sometimes in the evening and after 6pm that was when I was finally ushered into a small room and told to change into a garment robe and lay on the examination table. It was the doctor's young female assistant that came in and told me she was the one who was going to do the procedure and proceeded to do so. After-an-hour into the procedure, I thought I heard another voice (male) in the room with her and then it got quieter. And then half-an-hour later, I felt an arm shaken me to wake up and then everything was finished. Instantly I got up and felt woozy and off-balanced but managed to go into the bathroom and dressed-up. The only time I ever see Doctor Milvern was when upon leaving I was showed into her private office to sign some papers. And that was that! I made it back home from driving one and half-hour from Knoorblart to County Banque. Nothing happened and I did not feel anything wrong. It was by the "Grace of GOD" that I made it alive coming out of that clinic office. I always felt like someone from the job was following me and may have contacted with the doctor ahead of my arrival. It is like, you know, when you get this strange vibe or hunch and you completely ignore it, well it came back to bite me "Big Time". Right in the Butt!

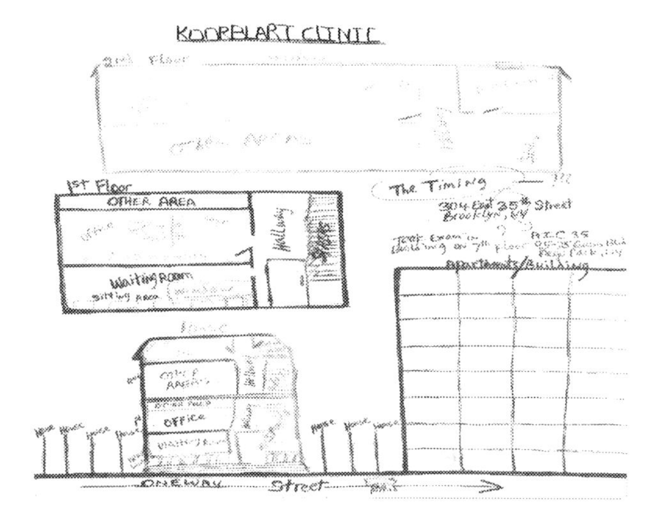

Figure 3

No wonder people were starting to wonder if I was a flake? By GOD, how I came back from the" Abyss" still mystified me? What was in my system? One way it got there was from that Knoorblart Clinic Office of Doctor Milvern. Boy-oh-Boy! Did she do a colonoscopy on me? My motto is, "What goes around comes around?" I do not know what **Hypocritical Oath** she took but I do believe it goes something like this, **"First and Foremost Do No Harm!"**

Still, it is even bizarre as a doctor to have that kind of a mindset. What kind of a person think that someone needs to be focused from the rear when a person came in for medical reason as to alleviate a condition with difficulty in excretion? Wow!!! What a female? Very, very interesting gauche of the female species.

CHAPTER V
THE MEMORIES

The Conscious Versus The Subconscious. Memory is the ability to recall information at will, thus memory comes and goes. What is fascinating about memory is that what is pleasant, we tend to remember but what is too painful, we tend to suppress? How amazing it is that one's mind can filter out what information it needs to preserve and process?

Dated: June 18, 2007

THE PREMIUM BOAT CRUISE

May 1999

The Itinerary: Consists of two hotels stayed-in, one in Lankcome and the other was in Doranzoo during the $2,000.00 getaway trip. My mindset at the time was to get away from all the disarray, needless to say there were other agendas skewing along without my knowledge. Someone was stalking my every move and now my life has become a disarray. Pertaining to the $2,000.00 requested from the Stout's Office on 04/22/99 which got duplicated on 09/21/99 by the same amount $2,000.00 in the Frantz's Office was always a weird and a nagging feeling in the back of my mind. This is the same Stout's representative that took those 1997 Christmas Party pictures where for some flute reason, as many times as I have asked her for my pictures, she dumbly replied they do not exist. The pictures in question, were about me in a red dress (full length to the ankle) with the red scarf embroidered with gold stars and this loose of a Spanish Woman (at the time had no knowledge of her disposition) wearing the purple dress (knee length). Why would Stout's representative go to this length to fabricate a salacious story that would adversely affected the function of the company is still questionable? To played me for a laughingstock was at best, a tremendous downfall for them because "What goes around, comes around?" I remembered specifically, I was told that the fur coat that I was wearing that night and into the late night at the Starlight was faux. Wow, that was real genius of him to comment on that. I may have worn an outer faux material that night; but my interior was as authentic as that faux blondness attitude displayed that night. I was truly genuine but what about being a dumb blonde. Do not get me wrong, I do not like to stereotype people, but there comes a point in life where one must take a stand and say enough is enough. What give some people the leverage to disparage other groups based on their differences while having the time of their life with no regard to the consequences? When a person is down, the best thing to do is to give them a helping hand, not to rub salt in their wounds?

"Whatever Floats Your Boat?" Is to either sink or swim? I went into the boat → and I got floated. I remembered feeling seasick and I asked for some remedy to calm my sickness and they gave me those "Pills". There were three (3) pills in a packet and I end up taking two on the boat and had one left. Now I am pondering what were in those pills? I seriously do not think they were really seasickness prevention pills. Because I am extremely careful of timing my activities and vacations with my monthly cycle that I should not have had it when it came for it was scheduled to come a week later after my vacation. That is why, everytime I have flash back memories of the cruise, I wondered why it came sooner than later and right after I took those pills. I was taught not to eat, drink or take anything from strangers that I am not familiar with. There and then, I let my guard down!

NOW, the third hotel we stayed-in was at the Palace INN, never heard of it, until someone thinks that they can have the authority to play King of the Jungle with peoples' lives. My moto is, "Do Unto Others As You Would Have Done Unto You". I am quiet by nature, but mess with me and you mess with the wrong person. Holding a Publishing Company and TV Network to have an avenue to do whatever you feel is necessary in degrading, disparaging, endangering, and insulting an enemy just to suit your big ego, is by far your prerogative, but when you step over the line, and mess with someone's life with the intent of criminal activities, then it becomes my prerogative. Again, my moto is, **"To each his own"** and not the other way around, what is mine is readily yours. Who are you to keep what is mine when we were nothing but business acquaintances? Maybe in the past, your royal treatment of others is widely accepted, but you met your match when you mess with my life. I am Dire Quotidian, better known for my mysterious disposition and the wonders I can do. As you would like to make fun of people with special needs/disability, then stick this into your pipe and smoke it by learning to address a person by their correct name? And by the same token, you are very lucky I did not "FooFoo" you. As life taught us all a valuable lesson, each one is an individual. What is good for the goose is also good for the gander?

Later, during the Dinner Table that first night, I conveyed to the waiter that I was suffering from seasickness and would not be able to eat. The waiter then brought me a small package containing three (3) tablets of seasickness pills to combat the illness. I took only one that evening and brought the remaining two back home with me. My cousin instead got the patch in the form of a bracelet (I should have done the same). Nothing bad happened, I felt find afterwards.

CHAPTER VI
FREEFALLING

Full Disclosure: Year 2000.

The Whirlwind Of An Abyss. Whoever said freefalling has and an end don't know about the "Abyss Of My Life". Sometimes in March and early in the morning, as I was leaving to go to work, I got extremely sick, weak and dizzy that I collapsed and fell from the top of my front steps and landed on the bottom step of my house. I got up and drove myself to work as if nothing seriously bad had happened. Needless to say, at first, I thought it may have just been the sun in my eyes that caused me to fall but the underlying fact was that my body was beginning to react to whatever ailment hiding within from that medical procedure in 1999. The "Stench" seeping out from my pores. Nothing can be done to get that "Stench" out, no matter how many showers I took, scrubbed, perfumed, and all, nothing works. This was the beginning of my freefalling and what to come of it. Had I known then what I know now, I should have gone to the hospital immediately, but I did not know anything nor suspected anything was wrong?

After persistent not feeling well, I went to see the doctor on April 1, 2000. He did the overall routine checks-up, requested lab-works and recommended various tests for blood and urine. My metabolism and physiology were working overdrive and yet nothing showed in my blood stream nor in my urine. Still, that did not prevent me from getting sicker and sicker and to the point where I could not function anymore.

Then by May 2000, two and half weeks into the new job, I had to say goodbye to the company and hand in my resignation at Mitrance Corporation. Afterwards, going forward was next to impossible, felt like airy, spacy and time capsule in my head. My body was physically moving but my mind was in and out of focuses. Here and there, I would get a glimpse of something and then just as fast as it came, that is how fast it would go away. Depending on the phases of life, one moment I might be in cognitive and the next, I am in La-La-Land, nothing was registering.

AFTER LEAVING MITRANCE CORPORATION: YEAR 2000

My health was deteriorating at such a rapid rate that for the first time since that occurred, I got really scared. I am getting nauseous all the time. Vomiting at interval. The headaches are back. My tongue has pink patches about three spotted pink patches two on the leftside of the tongue and one on the rightside of the tongue. It is after seeing my tongue that I became really scared for myself and finally admit to myself that I am really physically sick, and my health is deteriorating really fast. On my left buttock I felt a real big lump on the bone itself. On my right ear at the back and on the bone, there is a lump. Both of my legs skin surface is shriveled and wrinkled. And my right hipbone is extremely sensitive and radiating pain when touched with pressure. And last but not least, on the inset of my right leg where the top of the femur meets the hip socket, there are three lumps.

THE HALLUCINATION
(Felt Like Living A Nightmare)

1. Objects magnified
2. Memory Lapsed (Lost of Memories)
3. Normal Sounds Seemed To Be Loud → Ringing In My Ears
4. Head Spinning →Dizziness-→Severed & Prolonged Headaches
5. Panic Attacks → Easily Startled

6. Afraid Of My Own Shadow → Always Looking Over My Shoulders
7. Could not Be In A Crowd Of People → Suffocating
8. Constantly Falling With No Warning→ Approximately (3-4) Times
9. Repeating Things
10. Tired and Fatigued All The Time → Heavy Sleep

HEART

1. Mild Pain Shooting-Up To The Left-Side Of My Chest With Burning Sensation And Stinging.
2. At Times It Harden With Pricking And Sharp Excruciating Pain That Made It Hard To Breath.
3. Racing Heartbeat.

STOMACH

1. The Sight, Smell And Taste Of Foods Made Me Nausea.
2. Could Not Keep Anything Down/Unable To Eat.
3. Constant Upset Stomach And Aches.
4. Frequent Diarrhea And Constipation.
5. Stomach, Virus And Bowel Movement.

JOINTS AND MUSCLES

1. Numbness And Stiffness To The Arms And Legs.
2. Knees Swollen → At Times Painful When Kneeling.

SPEECH/VOICE

1. Inarticulate / Incoherent.
2. Babbling Like An Idiot.
3. Inaudible Sounds (Lost Of Speech).
4. Coarse And Hoarse.

SIGHT/ SOUND

1. Seeing Things That Weren't There (Dark Shadows; Creatures).
2. Hearing Muffling Sounds, Hissing Noises.
3. Blurring Visions → Objects Moving About.

SKIN TONE

1. Discolored With Dark-Reddish To Purple Spots On Both Legs (PURPURA).
2. Shriveled Of Both legs.

OVERALL HEALTH

1. Exuding Strong Body Order
2. Rotten Eggs / Rotten Meat
3. Fishy Smelly
4. I Stunk Like The Sewage
5. Burning Upon Urination

On June 5, 2007,

Something remarkable happened. Now, I understand why it was crucial for me to have the need to put to words all that I had experiences. When I first sat down to write my journal about all my trials and tribulations, I did not know it would have become a sort of therapy for me. Oh Boy! Did I need it! If I had not been prepared for what to come, I would have gone into a major shock today? But I remain as cool, calm, and collect as possible. I would have folded and buckled under. There is indeed such a thing as a parallel universe. How two people can have very different lives yet somehow to live the same experiences at the same time?

In any event, what I say about a "DÉJÀ VU" really does exist. It is like pieces of fragments of my life being put back together into whole. I have a creative mind and I can readily script a novel but never something as unbelievable as the truth itself and as incredible as it may sound, the whole text is the truth. That is why seeing is believing.

The infamous letter that I had written to seek help and get some resolution never did its job. Maybe I should have screamed louder. I know I appear much younger than I am, but I am wise beyond my years.

Indeed, there are two sides to a story and the truth. Sometimes, stories are facts taken out of contexts and concocted into lies that take on a life of its own and become the truth. Back then, I did not even have an inclination that a parallel universe existed. Why I wrote this, I do not know? In any case, it did not do much to help the situation. The mind games that they were playing. But regardless, first thing first, back now to today's episode when I first saw the doctor, he kind of looked familiar. But when he spoke, I did not recognize the voice. As shocking as I was to see him, I kind of sensed that he was just as shocked to see me. The man I remembered is much older looking therefore it could not possibly be the same person. Why not? I for one, look much younger than I started with after 911, but if what I am guessing is true, he too, can look much younger than what he started out with. In any case, I showed no reaction and remained as stoic as can be, for now, nothing can surprise me anymore. To experience what I have experienced, it would take JESUS, Himself to surprise me.

Maybe the doctor is the person I think he is. Just as I looked like my mother but a younger version, he too, might looked like his father but a younger version. Boy, he looked very, very familiar. I am not surprised that the encountered took place, for eventually, everything was leading to that moment. Why do people feel necessary to play hide-an-seek game with me? Aren't we adults here? Am I the only one who is mature in all this hogwash? A simple straight forward question that would require a "yes" or "no" answer is suffice to me. I would have been forthright. There is no need to go round-about-ways just to elicit a reply from me. Because I am as straight forward as it gets. No wonder I easily get annoyed!

Therefore, it was crucial for me to write my own stories in my own words as I know it well for, I had lived the nightmares and all. No one can tell my story better than me. But it would have been interesting to see what the other version is, as I do believe that a possible parallel story exists somewhere. If I was lured into the One World Trade Center on that unfateful month, maybe he too was lured into it under false pretenses. Then it is possible that he survived as I survived. Hence, the "DÉJÀ VU", talked about earlier.

Now something been bothering me for the longest time, and therefore I am guessing it could have been that Nagging Feeling again.

It was while in the new company Mitrance Corporation that I was first contacted by a recruiter named Mr. Darcy Potts.

The Restaurant Encounter. The Diner Episode - On Carterol Road (year 2000)

At that time, it never dawned on me why it did not click in that moment that I was so close to my former Job in Mammoth Court? Was it the start of lapses in my memory? To be so close and still be so far away and not realizing that the "Diner" from across and opposite the Centre Mall was indeed within distance from my former job.

Prior to the meeting, the only time I have ever been to the area was in 1992. Why do some people think that they can play with other people lives? Also, that is the connection with Maynard Central. The first time I corresponded with him was answering back his letter that I had received from him back when I was at the Mitrance Corporation. Even then, something was always nagging at me, and it was not until many years later that all this made a lot of sense.

The 2001 computer switched must have started with this switch. Come to think of it, he did classify himself as being a wiz mathematician and an expert in technology and the art. How did he get his hands on pertinent and very private information is something to be figured out? The most relevant piece of information that should have alerted me was when said person knew my family members. How was that possible, should have been a red flag for me? I am here about business transactions but all he was doing is questioning me about the books that I have read which at the time made no sense to me as I thought it to be very peculiar. I did not know it at that time, but could it have been, in June when I went to the main library in Quelchetown County and took out those three books that someone was watching me. It absolutely reinforced my notion that I must have been watched from the beginning and how creepy to think it now? I do have a six sense. Just thinking about it gives me the creeps.

Then in year 2001, I got this called to go to "The City" and that is when my jewelries were stolen. If I can recall exactly, there was an episode from one of those books about jewelry thieves, along with switching identities. And guess what, same thing happened to me. The subway incident happened because of the beginning of the year when I attended the New Year's Celebration in "The City". Did not know it at that time it was the beginning of my hell?

It must have been toward the end of the month of May, when Mr. Darcy Potts scheduled an appointment to meet with me at a restaurant in the area.

EN ROUTE: Appointment Time 8:00AM

Arrival Time 8:30AM

I left my house at a decent time in order to arrive at the Steakhouse that normally would have taken me 45 minutes to one hour.

➔But on that morning, it rained heavily, and it came down like buckets of water. I barely could see the signs on the road as it got dimmer and shadowy. To make matter worst, that snob of a man gave me the wrong direction which led me to make the wrong turn as I got off the highway. Thus, I was heading in the opposite direction when I came by a car with two men on the roadside. One by the driverside and the other at the trunk, outside in the rain, soaking wet.

I rolled down my passenger-side window and asked them for directions. They told me that I was heading in the wrong direction to make a U-turn and keep going up. They watched me to make sure that I was going in the right direction.

➔Since, I was so far down when I went the wrong way, I kept driving up and never seemed to find the place. Luckily, I spotted a payphone in some vacant lot, whence I stopped and called the restaurant. A woman answered the phone. When I asked her for information about how to get to the restaurant, she then asked for my location to where I was calling from. I replied to her question which at that point, she told me that I was just about ½ mile to where the restaurant was. (Because I had gotten out of the car to make that phone call, I was soaking wet from top to bottom.)

Then comes the DIRE SOFTWARE.

People Lives Are Real Not Something To Make Believe.

(All this time it never dawned on me the significant of the Dire Software until now August 17, 2013. I had had in my possession the Dire Software Disc when I had the Masterkeys for the 1999 Toyota Car.) But I threw it away back in December of year 2006 because I wanted to welcome the New Year 2007 without any distractions. Months later in year 2007 I had a change of heart and called the sanitation department to retrieve a loss item. No such luck!

MILLENNIUM: YEAR 2001

On top of that, the white woman with the medium blond hair behind the glass counter office resembled the white woman seating directly behind me on the bus with the short-cut blond hair. Now to think of it, I wonder if they were the same person, for both women resembled one another as in an older and a younger version of the same people. The importance of the "Vision" was like an eminent warning that the white clothed-man represented the purest of what to come had I stayed on the southbound side of the street and not moved to the northbound side of the street as in a parallel transition. The double-likeness of the two white women represented the darkness of deceits as in a natural transition. The computer-switch (two computers), the data manipulation, the reversal number 3 into the letter E, the tagging and the Identity Theft. I did not stand a chance to their "trickeries" for I became oblivious to my surroundings. It was not until after-the-fact that everything came into focus as one is in hindsight rethinking every moves and steps taken?

The September 11, 2001 that happened stayed forever in my mind. It all started with the wild goose chase to an interview in the One World Trade Center Tower. I can never forget that day and what happened afterwards during the two weeks before and after leading to the 911 Catastrophe. How I almost became a statistic?

CHAPTER VII

TRADING PLACES [EXCHANGE PLACE]

After Some Semblance Of Lucidity Coming Back To Me, I Tried To Take Action By Putting My Life Together.

Dated: 05/07/07 - Why would not those two police precincts 415th and 270th file the papers? I brought in the documents!

After numerous telephones calls to both precincts and trying to rectify matters over the telephone, I finally went to both precincts myself. First, I went to my local precinct, the 415th Precinct whereby I was given a manual procedural instruction sheet to follow. Second, I went to the 270th Precinct in County Banque to report suspicion of Identity Theft. I boarded the bus from my house to the last stop and transferred to another bus travelling to the 270th Precinct to file a written complaint report. The sergeant at the desk took the information and told me to wait for the credit bureau to answer my request and then come back to them with any new information. I felt like I was going around in circle for neither would react without the other one first.

FIRST INTERVIEW

On THURSDAY, April 5, 2001 – In the beginning of that week, I had received a phone call for a potential job prospect, to go to TELFRUS STAFFING @ The Exchange Place.

Accordingly, on that date, being unfamiliar with The Exchange Place location between Throad and Slinger Street, I made sure to leave 30 minutes extra in advance in the event I got detoured. Along the route and following specific instructions to (stay in the front cart) as I made my way to the next train connection, I got off the Gunhole Dropstop to take the Numbers Train going to Waykrauss Street, when the uncomfortable headaches started all over again? I was confused and getting disoriented as I waited on the platform for the train to arrive and it was getting late. I tried to call ahead to relate the fact that I was running late and that was when the **manipulation/exchange** took place. Looking around me, I saw the nearby subway public telephone and I went to use it and put in my quarter then dialed the Interviewer's number but the other line hung-up on me.

Then I tried a second time, but no pickup. That was when those two crooked people (a woman with a younger man) approached me, saying "Can they helped me?" I replied "no" to them but the two unsavvy people still hung around for a while but at a distance. The only time that they were so close to me was when they had asked to help me, and I got distracted in that moment. I quickly backed away from them, as they were that close in my space. After that, they kept their distance from me and from there that they were observing me, and "that was all the interaction I had with them." Finally, on my third phone call to the office, I got through to the other party-line and reached a person who told me that the interview was still on and they would wait for my arrival. Then the train came, I boarded the train and got off the Waykrauss Street Stop and walked the distance, turned some corner and came to the office building. No! Noone followed me on the train nor as I got out of the train. I went right into the lobby, where there was a sign-in/attendance sheet, I signed in. The old gray-haired Blackman attending the desk was courteous. He told me to take the elevator to the 10X floor. I got in the elevator to the

10X floor, stepped out and waited awhile in the open sitting area along with some "unusual characters". Then this young black woman, named Denisa, came and introduced herself as the person to see and asked for my resume. It was while I was reaching in my big bag to retrieve my resume to hand over to her that I noticed that my beautiful Gold Seiko Watch missing. I was frantic, started searching everywhere in the bag for it, but no watch. I just knew that the state of mind that I was in at that time, I would not have made an effective interviewer. Thus, after handing her my resume, I told the woman that I had to excuse myself for that day to deal with an unexpected emergency of losing my watch. She said fine and said to give her the resume just in case. I gave her the resume and went back to retrace my every step looking for my lost watch. Maybe, she too recognized the state I was in and thought that I would not have been an effective candidate as well. (In hindsight, I thought that the situation was nice with that woman for rescheduling the meeting and giving me another appointment for the day after, which was Friday, April 6, 2001) only to have everything in me screaming "nooooo" don't go back there. I thought it was un-daunting that those two goons of people in the subway had me as their focused target. Then I went about my way to retrace my previous steps and it was then I noticed my beautiful Rubies/Diamonds Pyramid Gold Ring went missing also along with the beautiful Gold Seiko Watch. When I came back to the lobby where the old Blackman was sitting, I asked him if by any chance he saw a watch fell, he said "No"? Then I went outside the building and started the search as I walked back my steps, nothing. I asked almost anyone and everyone I came across the street if they happened to have seen a watch on the sidewalk, still nothing. Finally, I went back inside the subway, and asked the booth clerk, if anyone reported finding missing items today, and she replied, "No, not today." Then I told her that I had lost some items on my way here and where can I go to find **"lost-&-found"** items. She then told me to wait a day or two for anything to come in. Then she wrote down a telephone number for me to call on a strip of $100 dollars money wrapper. She also told me that their **"lost-&-found"** was in the lower level of the Mezzanine on Gainne Street Station. I called numerous times and got nothing but the run around. The items were of sentimental value to me. I never did get any result, just a lot of run around. Those two items remained forever lost and so is my sentimental value (only GOD knows their true worth to me, no not the nominal but the sentimental attachment). Needless to say, I called that Friday of the appointment and cancelled. I just did not feel comfortable to go back to that same scene again. I felt uneasy that day. Now, the strange thing is, sometimes in year 2003 or 20004, when I went with my sister to hand in my resume at the Port Blanc Hospital, the old Blackman with the huge crucifix around his neck sitting at the medical office room looked very familiar (possibly that of the man encountered in the vicinity of the Waykrauss Street area back in 2001). This older Hispanic woman with hair pulled back retrieved my resume from me. She told me that she will file the resume along with the many received today. (I kind of got the impression that she will file my resume in the garbage.) From what I have gathered, it did not seem much resume came in that day. Oh, well! It is another way of filing unwanted stuffs into the disposable. It is amazing how one can detect the professionals from the nonprofessionals.

(After that, it took me many, many, many years later to go down into the subway again**. See Chapter 27)**

<u>SECOND INTERVIEW</u>

I am sensing similarity here with Ms. VaultPix's Meeting.

<u>Now The Real Issue At Hand: Dated Tuesday, June 26, 2007</u>

At the Consulting Company, I was contacted sometimes after the situation with 911, year 2001 to early in year 2002. I specifically spoke with the Ms. VaultPix, of said company in "The City". For some strange reason or another, she became attached to me like a concerned matriarch worried for a lost soul. I have neither met her nor have I known her from before. In any case, I did keep in touch with her as I was looking to get back on my feet pertaining to finding a job. The reason for this memory to come to me now is that, like my visions, a message is being transmitted to me. I remembered, being scheduled for an interview but could not remember the details pertaining to this account, until today when I got lucky and found the piece of paper with

◆◆◆

the written information that I have been searching for. The actual scheduled appointment for September 11, 2001, via a telephone conversation with Ms. VaultPix. The meeting was to take place at 110 Madgnet Lane –on the 82nd Floor and to report to Nebline Basset at The Financial Industry in Waykrauss Street between Gold and Slinger Street for a Specialist position. I was told to take the IRT Numbers Train to Fortburn Street or Waykrauss Street and walk toward Bellotteway down to Towville Place. The thing is, although I did not go to the meeting, I did not know it then at that time, but my gut and my instincts were telling me then something was not right at all. I called that morning and cancelled the appointment. Then I phoned Ms. VaultPix and told her, I had cancelled. For some strange reason, she got very furious with me and that is when she told me to write to Nebline Basset about not being interested with the interview. I did just that, wrote the letter and mailed it to Nebline Basset. Beforehand, Ms. VaultPix wanted to see the format of my letter to Nebline Basset, I was to fax it over first to her for a preview and then mailed it afterwards, of which I did. The thing is that, every time something bad almost happened to me, it always seemed to circle around the vicinity of the Waykrauss Street area. Tying that to the supposedly interview at The Exchange Place in Waykrauss Street, where I lost my Beautiful Gold Seiko Watch along with my Beautiful Rubies/Diamonds Gold Ring.

[Now, that brings me to another Tuesday at the Quelchetown Library in County Banque as I stood in line to be assigned a computer, that this old woman with a walking stick got snooty with me and just walked out of the line (That time, I felt that it was staged now I know why?) the old woman with the cane (walking stick) looked familiar, like Ms. VaultPix disguised. That is when I was assigned the #4 Computer against the wall and opposite it is #8 Computer. Funny thing happened, the girl using the #8 Computer stayed for about 5 to 10 minutes and then left (right then and there I felt something strange as if those two Computers were linked together) because that is when the **lewd POP-UP** appeared on my Computer and that nasty letter with reference to Parcekel Boulevard working part-time. This incident took place on January 29, 2002 at after 2:30pm.]

THE UNESSENTIAL INTERVIEW

June 21, 2007

THE CANCER FOUNDATION

When I had received a request for donations to the above foundation, I was first, dumbfounded and at the same time both pleased and honored? As a woman, it was my pleasure to oblige. Then come to find out much later that there was more to it.

Now, how and when did this misconception applied to me is not yet determined, but for the absolute certainty, I am hundred percent healthy. My bosom buddies are just fine and could not be any healthier and perfect.

I am making an educational guess here to why the facts got distorted. I foolishly answered an advertisement in the year 1997 pertaining to a casting call for surgical breast care. When I was called, I thought that, I was going to be a guest speaker on women health issues, not became a candidate of folklore? Oh well, good deeds never get rewarded!

The Casting Call, referred by Langley Haptor on a Monday @3:35PM
in Central City
Outfits: Corporate Dress
Subject: Surgical Breast Care

Back to the casting setting: When I got there, I was given an application to fill along with some other papers with personal background questionnaire and my resume. I was dressed in black business suit (vest and skirt) with a white blouse. As I appeared in front of the camera and filming was in progress, I started reading the monologue as it was written. Something magnificent happened and this vision appeared before my eyes, maybe it was the lighting and its radiance illuminating everywhere that blinded me and I saw this figure flashed before me. I immediately went blank, could not speak and made no sense. I was babbling like a fool. If that was speaking in tongues, is anyone's guess as it is my own? I do not know how to speak in tongues. I never did. Maybe I can and maybe I cannot.

(*That was my entire acting debut for now.*)

In addition, my plan account with TAEPNA was compromised. Now the striking thing about this TAEPNA plan account, is that I had requested a loan from the plan on 4/22/1999 for $2K and the named signed-off is Wanda, now this original loan was sent to The District Office where the same original loan is signed –off by Catlyn Frantz on 9/21/1999 from the legal department. The conspicuous thing about the whole transaction was that a duplication had taken placed. Meaning, from the original loan amount that I had received, an additional same amount was taken out under fraudulent terms. In reality, the real total amount taken from the plan is $4K that is the original $2K plus the same amount drawn of $2K taken fraudulently. Somehow, finances were being dipped into by many hands. The plan account had become, a revolving door.

CHAPTER VIII
RECTIFYING THE MISCONCEPTION OF A TRUTH

DO NOT INTERFERE WITH MY LIFE and everything will come up roses. Stop your meddling, you, media naysayers and keep out of my private life and this rollercoaster of twists and turns will undoubtedly have a better outcome.

NOW GOING BACK TO THIS 1997 CHRISTMAS PARTY: I cannot help but to see the correlation between my Gold Seiko Watch and my Diamonds/Rubies Ring being stolen in the subway on my way to that never happened Waykrauss Street Interview for it was at Waykrauss Street, I was supposed to meet with my demise/disappear. In addition, things started to unravel especially on one particular day, Friday, December 15, 1997 the day of the Company's Christmas Party. The woman that drove me and came along to the party was in a rush to get out of the party and since she was my ride, I had to leave when she left, and she did not take me home but brought me to the Starlight in "The City". It was strange that we left early and in hurry, and she was kind of shaken up but said that she needed a drink and wanted to party. Therefore, I have a real funny feeling that whoever you are may have it. Therefore, please find a way to inform me of their whereabouts, as those items were of sentiments. If by some strange reason, you feel necessary to attach me to some episode that I am unaware of, by your crude insinuation of having me copying your favorite black and white composition notebook with details of some insidious scenes, I only did as I was told for the sake of a job. But it is too coincidental to have my life being affected that way. I went through hell and back. This can really change a person and especially their perspective of the world. I am meek and humble, but I am also “a force to reckon with”. Being “nice” does not necessarily mean I am gullible only that I am refraining from calling out your “stupidity”.

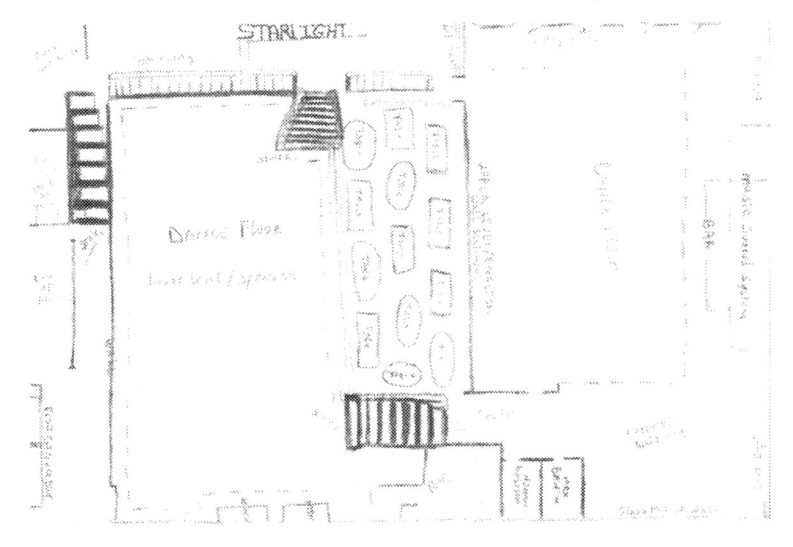

Figure 4

THE TRUTH

Sometimes the truths can be manipulated to fit certain criteria. If all the facts are not presented correctly, there is no doubt that lies are invented. A perfect example is the word known as an “omission”, which is a form of deception.

May 19, 2006: Discrediting A Person

To Discredit A Person is to make that person seemed unbelievable by way of either appearing to lose one’s mind; family history trait; or imaging things that were not there. Boy-oh-boy! I gave credit to my faith for some sense of reality and a keen mind that sorted things like a filing cabinet.

CHAPTER IX
THE DREAMS AND THE VISIONS

Dated: June 16, 2007

I Woke Up Late In The Morning From A Strange Dream.

I was in a gathering with mournful prayers. At some point in the procession, we had to form lines and advanced up front to the pulpit. I started in the 1st line, the very outmost line, but as I came to near the front of the line that I was in, I moved to the middle line on my right. That's when I was able to see clearly up front and saw that the line, I moved to was headed by a woman dressed in "avocado green gown" from top-to-bottom. Her head wrapped all the way around and the very long green gown that covered her entire body down to her feet. The 1st line that I had deserted was headed by a priest, dressed in his priestly outfit. When the priest saw what had transpired from the line, he was both saddened and disappointed with dread as he slumped down into a sitting position on the pulpit floor from where he was standing before? As I came to the very front of the line and standing before the woman on the pulpit, she asked me to recite some phrases after her. We started reciting, she first and then I followed. But along the way, the music that was playing in the background got louder and it became harder for me to hear the woman and I just mumbled not quite making sense. When the woman became aware of my mumbling, she got annoyed with me, and screamed from the top of her lungs for me to leave from her sight as I was not deserving to stand in her presence? I quietly replied to her that I knew everything, but she screamed at me and said "NO, and that I did not know anything". Then she said in a sarcastic way for me to recite the **"Our Father"**. As she forced my hands, immediately I straighten my body, stood tall, held my head high and recited the **"Our Father"** very loudly and clearly so that everyone can hear. The "avocado green gown" dressed woman was shocked to hear this and at the same time, the priest who had earlier slumped into a sitting position on the pulpit immediately stood up straight with a smile upon his face and continued with his line that now started to move forward. After I have confidently finished delivering my recital, the "avocado green gown" woman had no choice but to give me what she was withholding from me under false accusations.

My dreams always have meanings behind them. Some I can figure out readily, but others take me awhile at most, if not a longtime. In any case, they explain what had happened in the past and what to come in the present. I have a kind of a gift and if I am wise and use it accordingly, it might be beneficial and advantageous. The **Blessed Virgin Mother** appears to me in my dreams. Some of the revelations that she revealed to me in my dreams are profound and real. I found that out when days later what was shown to me in my dreams, really happened. Although, I tried to hide this manifestation within me, I cannot hide it from those who held this possession of true spiritual guidance. As I am a realist, I was not receptive to my ability at first and although many visions have appeared to me. It took me a long time to feel very comfortable with this special gift. Now is a matter of what to do with it. It saved my life!

June 26, 2007 – Tuesday

Today, I woke up feeling uneasy from not being able to fall asleep until late last night. Something was trying to come to my subconscious from accounts of past memories. I always believed that there is no such thing as mere coincidences. Also, to my advantage, I have a bad habit of always keeping notes and preserving information. Even doing my illness when I was unable to function at my full capacity, the training in me kicked-in and I was always keeping notes and being organized.

Dated: June 28, 2007

Sometimes Things Get Better Explained Through Dreams And Visions. A Déjà Vu Effect!

On Sunday, June 10, 2007, CORPUS CHRISTI day, I prayed to have the strength to walk the distance and my prayer was answered. I was able to walk the route taken all the way back to the church. How can nonbelievers do not believe, it is because, there is something lacking within them? I really felt a change coming over me. This is what cured me, my faith and belief. Throughout my illness that was all I lived on and went by along with some regular doctor check-ups.

MANY PILGRIMAGES: I have gone to so many Pilgrimages during the duration of my absentees that I cannot count them all. But one that stood out was, **The Rosa Mystica** (one of the many 42 facets of the **Virgin Mary**) that came to me in my dream and made this declaration (which startled me). "You haven't quite understood the significance of my "Mantle Robe of Protection" as I have given you the White Rose---reflecting the Purity given you when you were an infant being baptized, doing your First Communion, and into your Confirmation.

The Red Rose----reflecting the Suffering you took upon yourself when you set about and went on your own whence at time it got too much for you to bear and I eased your burden as I placed it in the middle of my chest.

Hence, the Golden Rose----is not yours to take yet for your heart is not as opened as mine. When you let your heart be as one and true, then you will know what I have always known?

Dated: September 16, 2007

Infant Of Prague!

Why did you leave me? Dream so profound and so real. But I left you in good hands, for Clavice Bruns was a nurse and plus the manager Dianne Wright was in attendance. "There is a child out there." "That must be reunited with his/her parent." Children often get lost in the system, sometimes lingering through a maze of bureaucracy that shifted them from places to places. Nonetheless, even the best intentions can go wrong!

Maybe that is why appearing to me in dreams, saying, "Why did you leave me?" Forever wondering who' s child was it? The strangest thing about the dream was the place it kept occurring and that was in the bathroom. I have been having strange dreams about the Bathroom Sceneries, for that reason, it brought me back to 1999 in the Company's bathroom.

The only bathroom incident that I am prelude to was that "bloody mess" in the Mammoth office at the job where Clavice Bruns pointed out to me as I walked into the bathroom upon my returned from my lunch-hour as I got ready to go back to my desk. I usually followed a routine that fifteen (15) minutes from my lunch-hour, I would go to the bathroom to fix myself up for I liked to brush my teeth, fixed my hair and face (loved to eat tunafish sandwich).

CASE OF KING SOLOMON: THE BABY FACTOR?

There was a Young Blond Woman from the legal department that was pregnant with child and she was four months much further into her pregnancy than her counter-part colleague who was still pregnant until December. The young blond woman gave birth to a baby girl. Then something dreadful happened, and I never saw her again after having heard that someone was pushed down or fell down the stairs with the "baby"??? I never saw her baby and I never saw her coming back to work in the office again. After the fall, the young blonde woman was rushed to the hospital by two good Samaritans that came to her aid, of which, one being her counterpart colleague who was also pregnant. That episode, I remember so vividly because it fell in line with the bloody mess in the bathroom in August 1999. **Whose baby was it?**

CHAPTER X

THE SIGNIFICANCE OF DREAMS / VISIONS

The Significance of my Dreams/Visions seemed to manifest itself in the daily and routine encounters with others.

Dated: October 2, 2007 - THE DISC

Confirmation Of Long-Ago Suspicion

An unfateful incident took place in East Quelchetown one day at Lateklis' Tax Accounting Firm where I was using his office computer and I inserted my Disc in the computer to retrieve a text document to make copies that my personal Disc got stuck inside his computer and I could not get it out. Mr. Lateklis told me then to leave it in the computer for awhile about few minutes and then he would see if he could retrieve the Disc from the computer. I did as he said for there was no way to pry the Disc out as it was getting harder with each try and would have end up with a broken computer. At that time, I did feel like he may have copied what was in the Disc, but I let go of my hunch and tonight, I got my proof.

(Items that were on the Disc→Songs, Prayers and Correspondences: 1) Thank-You God For My Being 2) I, Imagine 3) Free Like A Butterfly 4) Love

Is Really You 5) After Love 6) Rendezvous 7) Your F.B.Eye Agent 8) Here I Am 9) Deep In My Heart and 10) Together We Stand On Top In Love.)

Regardless, there is nothing he can do with them without my permission. As a supposedly Pastor, I shall give him "the benefit of the doubt". Using the "Bible" to take possession of one's creation is by far the lowest of the low. How does one respect such cowardice act? Had we had a conversation of his seemingly interested in my creation maybe then I can regard him as worthy but now that I have to put it all together myself to arrive at the truth, I found him to be untrustworthy and lacking in quality? The Power is mine, GOD gave me the Gift. Talking about being violated! That is invasion of privacy!

Personal and private thoughts are protected under the First Amendment. I firmly believed that while my Disc was stuck inside that computer, from the other end of the office with another computer, he was copying my information.

THE NORTHSWAYN ALMOST PERFECT SET-UP

Dated: July 10, 2010

While still in and out of phases, my former friend Crabeit who resided in Northswayn invited me to come to her hometown and get a cellular phone sometime in year 2000. It was the beginning and the birth of the cellphone. I drove the Solara, Toyota from my house in Quelchetown to her house in Northswayn in order to get that Cellphone. Strangely enough, looking back, we did not get the cellphone in Northswayn but instead we drove to another County Town to purchase the cellphone.

That afternoon, when I reached Northswayn, we went to FABB'S Warehouse to look at furnitures. She was interested in some new furnitures and I got taken by a beautiful china dinette set. When we got back to her house, she arranged it that I sleep in her son's room while she and her son slept together in her room. The next morning, she served me coffee with Chinese food, my favorite sweet and sour chicken. We decided to take my car for the journey to County Town and later, while on route to County

Town, I got very sick with severe diarrhea that we had to make a stop at the nearest public restaurant (MOMDUKE'S). I could not hold it anymore, I made a dash to the restroom and just relieved myself. If I did not go, it would have been right there in the driver seat of my car. (I never thought of anything then until now.) While in County Town and after the purchasing of the cellphone, we also planned to go to Baltnic, but decided against it as it had gotten way too late to travel in my car in the night.

Upon returning back home to Quelchetown sometimes a week later, I called to speak with her, but her attitude changed toward me. When I called her on the cellphone, and she answered me harshly saying I am making a "booty call"? That is the first time I ever heard such a phrase/comment. Since then I felt uneasy and never heard from her, gone by the way of Missing-In-Action (M.I.A.). Good riddance! (Turned out to be my Judas.) I am definitely a Dumb-Dumb. Wow! slow to learn, see and understand. Because I am not capable of perceiving such nasty deceit when it comes to children welfare.

OCTOBER 9, 2013 - R E V E R E N C E

This Wednesday coming home from work, as I went to reach for something on my small book stand that was in the corner in my room, my hand knocked over the **Rosa Mystica Statue** (one of the many 42 facets of the **Virgin Mary**) and what a surprise the piece of paper that I had placed under her footstool had been imprinted with the word REVERENCE on it as if to forever remind me that JESUS is seeking REVERENCE in a world marred by corruption, greed and assault.

It never failed, it was always the **Rosa Mystica** that revealed to me the **Majesty of GOD'S** way and his truth. If ever I have a revelation, vision or dream, it was always in the presence of the **Lady Rosa Mystica** as she was known for her many 42 different apparitions.

Why? Why? And Why?

◆◆◆

CHAPTER XI
THE NAGGING FEELING

The Story Lingers. Was It An Instinct, an Insight, or an Innate Sense That Won't Go Away? The Tell-Tale Of It All. This came after the "Exams". I just could not shake that nagging feeling off. Therefore, I needed a distraction, a get away!

"The Score", why won't the feeling go away? Somebody out there knew something about the score. I wish I knew then what I know now**.** In life they say, "things happened for a reason when no explanation can suffice". I say it is bulls—it. Nothing happens without a purpose. Be that as it may, what happened to me was calculated, criminal and near-death experience? Weird thing was that, I spent nearly twelve (12) years of my life not knowing whether I was coming or going. The same very words I used in my poems now I was living it. Unbelievable!

Since that "Un-fateful Day" on September 10, 2001 when I went to County Boulevard to take **"The Unforbidden Exam"**. An "Exam" I was totally prepared for. And just like that when I was being followed in Knoorblart on Friday in 1999, I was also followed to the examination building. The phone calls were already made, and the contact was already set, and the game plan was already in motion to **sabotage** the score.

Afterward, I kept waking up to that same **"nagging feeling"**, that just would not go away. I just needed a break from my surroundings and get away, so the cruise trip sounded good. Breath in outside air and clear my head. But, why was I so apprehensive before taking the trip - (May 1999)? It is true what they say about always listening to your gut feelings/first instincts.

This brings me back to the fascination with Bellotteway. What is this fascination with Bellotteway? (Wow!!! Little did I know it then that I will be back on Bellotteway 4/2013.) The only connection that I have with Bellotteway is that, I had attended commercial classes for ten (10) weeks on Bellotteway in 1997 given by Zeffings. Notwithstanding, this is when all those scooping and stalking started to and from between those individuals, and for some strange reason or another played a hand in my almost demise on that "un-fateful day" of September 11th, 2001 catastrophe. It took me a very long time to talk about that "day's" episode because I almost became part of it. Again, on August 28, 2001, I was sent on an interview in the One World Trade Tower, similarity, to the Waykrauss Street Area.

Dated: May 8, 2006: The Boat Cruise:

Why Did I Take The Cruise? After the "Exam"? I just could not shake-off that "Nagging Feeling" and in order not to dwell on it, I went on a Cruise Trip. It was a much-needed distraction. Normally, I am an upbeat person, and nothing can get to me that easily, but the "Score" →kept "nagging" at me and reinforcing in me that I am positively sure I had passed. The feeling just would not go away. In addition to, there were many other factors that I was dealing with at the same time, the funeral of a close-relative; the combat to save the dwelling place; the nonstop situation after another and so much more. I really needed a vacation – an alone time for me. What I have found out about myself is that, I have a knack to make difficult things seemed easy? The impossible, possible. All that is done through self-determination and hard work. Hence, I figured, why not reward myself for my major accomplishments? Yet, still that "Nagging Feeling" (I still believe in the "Score".) ***The crucial mistake I made, was to elicit the help of the wrong man. ➔hence for the "Letter".

THE OP-ED ARTICLE

There was a news-clipping of an Article in the Newspaper that depicted an OP-ED on a person of importance, concerning the rush to sign-off on 1100 pages of a user tax of "69% surcharge" on small businesses on the 11th hour after just finishing reading the budget bill.........which kind of fell in line with the "nagging feeling" of that moment when I knew I had passed the **"Exam1"**. I felt like someone knew the score and it was compromised. I always thought he was my "redsea" that was preventing me from crossing to my destination. A constant **"thorn on my backside".**

["THE SCORE", why won't the feeling go away? Somebody out there knew something about the score.]

CHAPTER XII
CHRONOLOGICAL

Dated: May 8, 2006

I don't know if it was the "Nagging Feeling" that irks me or the underlying truth behind it, in any event, I started keeping chronological listing of my past accounts.

The Time Frame - Sunday, January 17, 1999 to Sunday's evening, January 24, 1999.

- Sunday 1/17/99 - Not so sure about if she picked me up from my house or I met with her. She had to because I don't think that I would have carried around with me luggage (not so clear about that day of event).

- Monday 1/18/99 - Took the bus from around her house by the school and library then another bus transferred at the Mooteville Field Area Bus Depot to work. From work: I took the bus at my job to Mooteville Field transferred there for the bus to her house. Since I got off early and I was always early, I would go to the library each day and wait for her to pick me up when she got off from her job; that was the routine for the whole week.

- Tuesday 1/19/99 thru Friday 1/22/99 – same routine—always hitting the books for crucial study time.

- Saturday 1/23/99 – From morning until evening (even throughout my feverish sickness, I studied all day long. Then sometime midafternoon, her girlfriend came by and spent the day with us. I believed that she was either a nurse or nurses' aid because she too helped her friend Adleine St. Charles with the remedy that made me feel a little better. I felt a little better and to give me some relief from studying, by evening time they suggested we go out to relax a bit from all those cramming that I have been doing before the exam and I agreed. We, us three, took her jeep to the train station by her house and got on the train to "The City". It was raining that evening.

- bit from all those cramming that I have been doing before the exam and I agreed. We, us three, took her jeep to the train station by her house and got on the train to "The City". It was raining that evening.

We went to some club in the city named "SOB". As we came out of the subway, walked a few blocks on the same side of the street and then we went down the stairs to the lower bottom of a corner building on that street – the Club. It was a nice atmosphere; well-behaved patroness; and the band was playing on the stage. We took a table by the stage. As sick as I was, I made the most of it. I ordered one drink – margarita.

(On social occasion, I always tried to loosen up a little.) I enjoyed the music and after a while, I went on the dance floor and danced once by myself. Then someone came and danced with me.

Just that one drink I ordered and drank that night. I did not order any food for I would not have been able to keep it down as sick as I was, and that was all that happened that night at the Club. We stayed awhile and then we left, took the train back to the train station near her house and she retrieved her jeep from the parking lot, and we went back to her house.

- Sunday 1/24/99 – Got up and did some more studying and by evening she took me home. On our way to County Banque, she stopped at the Natwell Warehouse in Matzsaw.

The Time Frame That Shown Light To My Thought Processes At That Time And The Reason For The Flu Shot.

Tuesday 9/8/98 left at 2:30pm to the Amptauk – Friday 9/11/98 back in County Banque by 4:30pm

=I requested my vacation for the week of Monday 9/7/98 – Friday 9/11/98 from work.

Took the Upperhend Bus @ the County College bus stop to and from each time.

The ticket receipts, I gave it to Ms. Tartenron since it would get her some sort of a discount as she stated to me.

1) Tuesday9/8/98 – Left my house at 2:30pm to catch the bus at County College bus stop.
2) Wednesday – Thursday 9/9/98 – 9/10/98 – Got up and study all day and night long. Sometimes would stretch and took walks by the water.
3) Friday 9/11/98 – Study some more and came back home to Jamestown Village at around 4:30pm.

(*I did not go there for fun /went there to study ➔spent all those hours with the "books"*).

Proof of Passing Score for the "Exam"
Jaymart purchased item on 9/12/98 the Diamond Stud Earrings same day as the Exam date 9/12/98 Saturday.
*That's how sure I was of passing!!! See picture below of date of purchase, 09/12/98 Diamond Studs Earrings.

Plus, it was that "nagging feeling" that made me called and put in a request for "re-review" on October 27, 1998 – Tuesday.

➔Received the envelop/package information two days later October 29,1998 by the way was sent via "First Class".

➔I became discouraged from **"Exam1"** but regardless, I got upbeat and determine to prove it in the next test with **"Exam2"** which prompted me to take the course for better preparation.

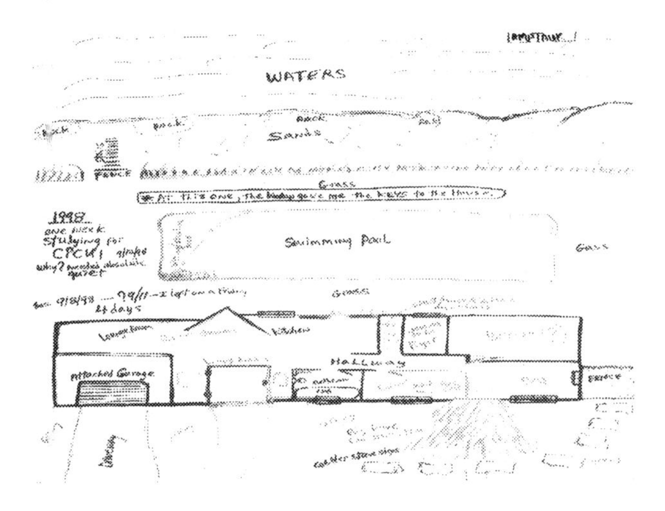

Figure 5

CHAPTER XIII

THAT IS WHY I HAVE BECOME "A FORCE TO RECKON WITH"

Having a scientific background gave me some insight to what incomprehensible, devious "funky", "dooky", "dungy", "sewage" manner of state that I was in? I, for one, am still amazed that I did not die and have come back to life. GOD is the ALMIGHTY! That is why, what human proposed, GOD disposed? Nothing can surpass his CREATION!

I went to see the doctor on the 1st of April. He took blood test and urine analysis and nothing showed-up in my blood stream nor in my urine. Yet, I am still getting sicker and sicker.

The Stench seeping out from all my pores.

How I went from being the "magnificent" Dire Quotidian to PePe-Le- Pew?

The chemical brew that almost changed my equilibrium, had taken more than twelve years of my life.

"PePe-Le-Pew" was the Infamous Cartoon Skunk. Now, if that does not stretch your imagination to what horrible nightmare befallen upon me than something is missing here?

Literally, I became so "smelly" that I could not live within my skin. That is why everyone was expecting for my "demise"? My metabolism was changing so fast from inside-and-out that both of my physiology and psychology were being affected.

The "perfect" Dire Quotidian has been transformed by cruel intentions. This is a criminal act that warranted prosecution. It took me more than twelve years of my life to get back on my feet.

SHELLSHOCK:

As far as I could remember, when something bad happened to me, I would first go through a shellshock episode and then I would become "A Force To Reckon With!" It is a delayed reaction instilled in me. My personal mechanism. It is my human nature. Cannot be stopped! I finally came to term with what it means to be "Shell-shocked". How tragic events can cause a person to blackout episodes and go into shock? It is amazing how one's psychic and inner strength can help one to cope. My goodness, I really did forget the nightmares I went through in Elementary School (6th Grade). Maybe that would explain why years later in my adult life, I wrote the prayer, "Thank You God For My Being" because at that time, I did feel like the end was near. **No one to turn to for help.** But in a strange way, I managed to pull myself through it and made it to graduation. It is all those memories that are coming back. Somehow, through it all, I always believed even when I could not see that someone was looking out for me. The concept that stated, "What does not break you makes you stronger" is so relevant in my present life today that it explained the self-confidence and the determination that I have built-up within me?

CHAPTER XIV

CHARACTER BUILD-UP

I Made It Through The Rain:

After what seemed like an eternity of going around in circles, something new came along and on February 21, 2009, I barked on a new endeavor and went to take the first Police Exam in "The City" at One Plaza Center.

This day today, February 21, 2009, I took the Police Exam for two and half hours (2.5 hours). Boy! Was it long and tedious? I don't know how I did but if I passed, it would be a miracle. During the Police Exam, my eyes got really bad and after staring for 10 minutes at a diagram of a crime scene just to memorize it later in answering the questions, I could not see out of the left-eye. I must have busted a nerve muscle for I got blood-shot-eye. At first, I thought it was the contact lenses in my left-eye but later, I remembered the incident from the night before when I was sweeping down the basement the particles got into my eyes. That night, my left-eye started to bother me, and I rinsed it off thoroughly with water, but it did not let up and the following morning, on the Examination Day, it got worst. Imagine walking around with one redeye. On top of that, when the sunlight hits the eye, it is as if all the muscles around the eye are being pulled in all different directions. What consequence to pay for with my left-eye when I was only trying to do a good deed? It really hurts! That is why, it had to have happened on the day before the Police Exam I reinjured my left-eye. All this hardwork with corrective lenses for my left-eye in preparation for the Police Exam that I ended up using just one eye for the Police Exam, in the end. Guessed what? I did not pass. It was meant to be, and I had a feeling that it would be so. I failed that damn Police Exam because of my own carelessness.

The second time I took the Police Exam again was at the Bunktowey Plaza in Quelchetown County.

1st Police Exam ➔ they failed me with 59 and gave me a Test Score of 69.411 – Coded #11. (I always thought it weird about the scoring system that they would fractionize it.)

ACTS 4:11 – This is the stone which was set at nought of you builders, which is become the head of the corner. (***from the King James Version (KJV) ----- The KJV is public domain and Copyright 1968***)

STAIRCASE TO MEMORIES

Dated: December 25, 2011 The CHURCH - CHRISTMAS SUNDAY

Fast Forward To The Present. I do not know if it is my subconscious mind talking to me or if it is "kaleidoscope of memories" surfacing back into my conscious mind. Either way, it is a revelation of possibly putting all the pieces together and completing this maze of my life. Maybe talking about The Centre Office and the combination of using the picture of stairs as a landscape to log-in into the system spurred up some memory, or maybe it is that "whacko woman" inside the "church" whom at I had sympathy for and thought there might be some good nature in her but actually turned out to be the devil inside the "church". I recalled something about her wanting to give me a paper/envelop to give to my mother and I had refused to take it from her and how ballistic she went off on me. Now it is December 25, 2011, I had gone to Mass as always on Sunday but this time I attended the next scheduled Mass (unfortunately, it felt like a comedic audition which made the Liturgy benile), in any event, that "whacko woman" named Monalee is definitely a thorn to the "church", a distraction and a disturbance to the word of GOD but it was the priest that allowed it and made whatever meaningful Sermons turned into a joke. The descending to the basement of the church lodge the notation of descending to the basement of The Centre Office where the Johnston Dove, Inc. was set up. There were total five of us (employees). Eventhough, the office was a confined space, I did like it and enjoy the job for it was fun. We ladies made it fun to work there. I recalled during my lunch hour how I would cross the railroad to visit the "church" there. Being there, I would find peace and serenity, as if something was calling me there. The door would always be opened, and I would walk inside the dark "church" and sat down at the end pews and started praying, and just like that, the lights would turn on. The priest would come out and set up the altar preparing for Midday Mass and so I would presume. Every time I would leave the "church" after praying, I always felt fulfilled, content and as if I am at peace. But then these unusual occurrences would happen; first the car accident; then getting ticketed for parking violations nonsense where I had to go down to the Town Hall Office (just so happened to be adjacent to the "church", right on the same block) to pay off the tickets. But never did I see a "whacko woman" in all this, perhaps there was always one there it was just that she was not as in plain sight as that Monalee. But in all this nuisance, one thing remains constant though, it seemed that they always come after me as if I have a target on my back. What gives? Now this "whacko woman" Monalee does not really know who she is dealing with because I have but tried my patience with her. She definitely does not know me from her "Eve's Rib" as I do not know her from "Adam's Apple".

Back To The Present Time! One particular Sunday of Mass, as always, that woman "whacko woman" Monalee did what she normally would do in the "church" making it a mockery, walking around the front of the altar, and talking out of turns. At the end of the Mass Celebration, as I was walking out of the pew I turned back to see where she was and there, she was on the folding chairs sprawling like a Cleopatra awaiting her Anthony. The last time I checked; I am in the Roman Era of Christ not in the Greek Mythology of Wackiness. They told me that "whacko woman" Monalee was a very educated and very well-versed elite woman (at first, I stood up for her while everyone was saying she was whacko) but now, I had enough especially when this annoying priest started turning the Pulpit into a joke. As educated "whacko woman" Monalee may or may not be, I Dire

Quotidian said she is not, because if she were to be, and even if she had some kind of maladjustment of the brain, there were certain things that one just does not do in REVERENCE to the Holiest of Holiness. Yes, "whacko woman" Monalee is smart in cunningness as Satan was in his wits to get at the very feeble minds. She can play on others sympathy and lack of savviness for the Catholic Religion, but I would like to stand toe-to-toe with her and watch her go down as the annoying pain that she truly is. I do not have to use a crystal ball, nor a palmreader, nor a psychoanalysis (creepies), nor a telepathy, I would just use the REVERENCE of my **Virgin Mary** and the Gifts of Prayers to reveal what a bluff that person is when there was no real substance to begin with except for the mere pleasure of intimidations and control. As the book of Revelation warned, beware of false prophets who prophesize in the Name of Jesus and yet cannot tell you who JESUS is? They are still grasping at the concept of "THE HOLY TRINITY in ONE". If one can just pass the façade of this "whacko woman" Monalee, one can decipher her true motive as playing the part of three in one person being educated, self-importance, senile person that is conniving in using her intelligence to manipulate, intimidate, and confuse the Catholic Community. One thing is for sure that she has going for her that others do not, is her keen knowledge of the "Bible". It is sad to see that she is playing the religion community like a fiddle and everyone falls in line to her tune.

THE INFAMOUS ENVELOP

I think I have figured out now who from my past is like a "whacko woman" Monalee in my life. Can it be "Flauluka"? You know what my motto is, "Out Of Sight, Out Of Mind". But, why now? After all those years, why now? Is it a grudge thing because I recalled that we left on good terms? Or maybe she was just as "whacko" as Monalee. I remembered all those different "whacko hats" she would wear and that "Infamous Reference Letters" of which I had asked her to compose for me to send to those Law Schools that I was applying for. Boy! Did she did a number on me, where she wrote that I was only good for a "Lingerie Model". (Is it not creepy that she had her eyes on my body?) Eventhough she may have destroyed my career path, I cannot say it was jealousy alone, but it must have been more than that? Afterwhich, I spent another seven months looking for a job until I landed one with Tigwa Co. Then after a year and one month later I was abruptly let go. Now I am wondering if that damn letter surfaces into Tigwa Co. repertoire. I used to believe in the saying that goes, "Naive Is Bliss". Well, not so true anymore! **Naivety is not a blessing, indeed no, it only prolongs the inevitable.** Still to my dying shame, I imagined all those "Infamous Reference Envelopes" circulating "The City" Law Schools.

Oh Boy! Talking about being slow, sometimes I am slow! When it comes to see what is in front of me, I just do not see it? It is always after the fact. When am I going to realize that being fast means sometimes, I would miss the "big picture"? Funny thing is that I prophesized it long before I knew it to be true, that "Life Has A Way Of Coming Back In Full Circle."

If I did not die is because I have an angel on my side?

This year, I definitely have my CHRISTMAS!

◆◆◆

CHAPTER XV

UNHEED WARNINGS CAN LEAD TO ADVERSE RESULT

FEBRUARY 2013

Sometimes in February of 2013, I had this unusual dream that I put off as being strange and weird but if I had paid close attention to it, I would have seen that it was a warning. The reason at first, I brushed it off was because of the person I dreamt about, Mardline. I knew of Mardline when I was in my teens (maybe 15), we were never closed or never bonded as a family. As a young girl, you go with your mom wherever she inclined to, and you did not have a choice in the matter and so that is how and when we were introduced as cousins. Now, the dream I had was that she appeared to me somewhere and said she wanted to tell me something and proceed to do so. She told me stuff about betrayal and that it was a person within the family, specifically warned me about Trebolt. I guessed I was not paying her any mind because she reprimanded me and said that I was stubborn and should have heed to her words. Even in dreams, the relationship one has in real life is also the relationship one has in a dream and that is precise. I basically knew of her but do not know her just like she knew of me and does not really know me.

I wished I had paid more attention to what she was saying and now, June 2013, as hard as I tried to recall the dream, it does not want to be remembered. Everything in me is sensing all that dreadful warnings are about to come to light. I never liked nor trusted Trebolt and I guessed I was not the only one. But the question is why Trebolt? Why not any other persons in the family? One thing I did right was to tell my mother about the dream, at least someone else besides me is aware of my dream.

CHAPTER XVI
DYNAMICS AT WORK

Tuesday, February 11, 2014: Glimpse Into Impasse

As often as I have taken the E train to the last stop – Phambolt Street? Or the A and C Trains passing Phambolt Street, I would see the pictures of the eyes on the mural (and nothing clicks) but today, for some strange reason, on my way home from work taking the E train, I noticed the eyes on the wall of the subway entrance, the stop behind St. Lauol's Church on Fortburn Avenue and close proximity to the World Trade Center Area. (I noticed it that morning on my way to the work and followed through with it at night on my way back home.) Now what played in my mind is the scene of someone coming out of that subway/stop station and be completed surrounded without an escape route. (Lord knows what treacherous, devious thing happened then.) I got goose bumps and the shakes all over. Something is irking at me. It is a lot of Kaleidoscope of memories that want to be put together. It always took a catalyst to make my mind go deep into that reservoir of memories and tried to remember things. Now the strange thing is nothing happened prior to today episodes and why is that? I started noticing and tracing these accounts in the earliest part of the morning as I make my way to work and the meeting. But the person that came in the meeting I have never met before and after work and going back in the same direction to take the E Train that "nagging feeling" and the shakes increases as if I am so close to discover the truth. That is my glimpse into the Impasse, whether I consciously or subconsciously holding back the memory because of the parallelism of a set-up to take a fall that I was oblivious too. Similarity must have also existed just like when I went through "hell-and-back", but I cannot even begin to compare the suffering of that "individual" becoming a prey to those vultures as they laid in wait for him coming out of the subway. Cannot fathom the nightmare that person faced! But who was the Good Samaritan? Right there behind St. Lauol's Church.

CHAPTER XVII

THE BIG PICTURE

Seeing is Believing. When seeing becomes unbelievable, then one's sanity becomes questionable? That is why seeing is believing to make sense of it all. Sometimes, you must pull yourself back and take a good look at the surroundings in other to assess it all.

What Is Wrong With The Picture? For things to equal, must find what is common between them.

DELIBERATELY TARGETED CAR INCIDENT ON SUNDAY, JUNE 18, 1999

Just about a month from purchasing the brand new car -1999 Toyota, on a Saturday, the weekend of July 17, 1999, I took my sister Jaxxime with me to the Quelchetown Furniture Store in County Banque (which was adjacent to the 973rd Police Precinct) to look and pick out a brand new set of Furniture Bed. The salesperson/showperson helped us with picking out the bed-set and we both took turn trying on the mattress. We liked what we saw and told them that I would be back tomorrow to make the purchase. The following day, Sunday, July 18, 1999, I went alone to the store and to make the purchase with my credit card.

Then going back to my car, I first made a stop at the Hot Dog Stand that was on the sidewalk. I crossed the street to the other side, opposite the Parking Lot to get there and bought a can soda (sprite) and put it in a brown paper bag and then went to the Big Parking Lot across from the library to where I parked my car.

Getting in my car and driving out of the parking lot unto the street, I came upon "Seventy-third Street", a one-way road going down Quelchetown and at the traffic light to make a left turn unto Jamestown Avenue. When the traffic light turned green, I proceeded and made the left turn unto Jamestown Avenue and continued forward, not soon after and not even getting far, just barely reaching 175th Street when it happened? I was side-swiped and hit by a parked-car coming onto the traffic into the street aiming right at my car. My first reaction was to swerve in order not to hit the car that was already in front of me. (Thinking about it and writing about it, felt like I was deliberately boxed in by those two cars to cause a chain reaction, which would have paraphrased the saying in the "Insurance Industry" as a CAT and MOUSE play). It was Dark Blue Four-Doors Car with one person inside, the female driver named "Jane Doe" (about 5'0-5'2"). Wheeling from the aftermath of being shocked, frozen, stunted by what just happened to this brand-new car, when it was just about a month old. I carefully drove my car in front of hers and parked alongside the sidewalk right behind hers. She too, stopped and parked her car in front of mine. We both got outside of our respectively cars and talked briefly, afterwhich, she gave me some bogus identification, some ID with her name as "Jane". (She said something to the fact that her mother was in Central City sick and was in hurry to get there) and left the scene. Just in that instant, about a minute past when a police car drove by my car and just looked at me. What the F-U-D-G-E? This is a brand-new expensive car that were talking about here. I was still standing there frozen, dumbfounded and stunt by the damage done to my new car.

OPINION: I think that one of the cops occupying the police vehicle that had passed by me on that day after the incident may have actually been earlier inside the Furniture Store as I recognized him to be the one in the passenger seat. Humm, the cops are from 973rd Precinct.

ERROR: My error was that, I went to the 415th Precinct in County Banque instead of the 973rd Precinct in Quelchetown where the accident actually happened. (Went to the wrong Precinct to file a claim). That is why the woman cop said she could not help me because her computer showed no record of such. (???Here I go again, chasing my tail all over again???)

[Hence, the driver license picture tied into the car incident being deliberately targeted on July 18, 1999 on Quelchetown Avenue. Of course, the Department Of Motor Vehicle is right on top of the 973rd Police Precinct. I always felt it was much more than that, but I could never pinpoint anything when you only have pieces and pieces and pieces of information. Kaleidoscope of information. When memories collided with facts, that is when all the pieces come nicely together?]

THE VORTEX – TYING THE MISING LINK

On November 21, 1997 per a former colleague Bradston's bequest from my old job, I got introduced to Arts/Paintings that she was personally involved as a side-job at the Art Company in her residence at Knottville, NY to sell to the public during a "House Event Gatherings". I bought one painting from the salesperson during the presentation, it was the "Floral Portrait". Hence, my information such as my address and phone number were with them in their system. Afterwards, all hell starting to break loose such as, my car being targeted in the parking lot at the job, my desk/computer being sabotage in the office, and I was being followed.

04/18/08 THE CAR 1999 CAMRY SANDRIFT

Saturday, April 12, 2008**à** passing by the church on my way to class, the landscaping / lawnmower guys said something about "baby." Now that got me "thinking" that it seemed that this whole mess seemed to congregate about the Toyota, Sandrift Car. I remembered the incident with the Baby and the 8 years old Boy in the car and the screw puncturing the tire. Now to think of it afterward, the Toyota became weird to drive and function →like it was bugged or something.

Sometime after the incident, which weighted heavily on me, the endangerment of a child/baby. I became distraught for every time I would see a baby, the flashback of memory pops-up of many **"WHAT-IFS?"** swirling around in my head.

One afternoon, I remembered driving over to friend's house in Knottville and rambling about "baby/baby", I know I was not making any sense back then but now I wondered if I was being recorded and the thing is that at that same time, her little girl about 2 years old was playing around with a soiled diaper. I kept thinking when my friend was going to change the Baby's Diaper. It happened on a Thursday Afternoon/Evening outside int the driveway of my friend's house.

My car in her driveway. We were outside talking. The attached garage door opened with her little girl inside playing with a toy wagon/pulley in a soiled diaper.

The car had to be bugged for the conversation to be recorded.

CHAPTER XVIII
WITH THE TOUCH OF THE HANDS

Yes! There are HEALERS out there, that have the LAYING ON OF HAND. Miracles are being done all the time but let us not confused **"True Healers"** from **"False Sorcerers"** practicing black-magic.

I can attest to that! At some point in my life, during my tumultuous years I did manifest the ability of the "Laying On Of Hand". I first noticed this ability when going to Church and during mass, the priest would ask the congregate to reach out and shake each other hands to show the **"sign of the peace"**. When I would reach out and touched peoples' hand, I would have preview to realm of insights that at times could be scary and other times revealing? I could no longer stand the sensation that I was getting hence, I would not shake people hands anymore. Little did I know it then there were other peoples with that kind of "Revelation" like me.

My first encountered was with my eye-doctor who literally saved my left eye. But he is too modest and would not hear of it. I should know because on February 21, 2009 while sitting in an opened auditorium waiting to take "The Police Exam, this bright light out of nowhere hit my left-eye (mind you, we were indoors). When we were finally allowed to enter the exam-room, and in the middle of the exam process, I felt this sharp pain in my left-eye followed by stabbing sensations to the nerves in my left-eye. I had to promptly leave the room and go the bathroom to wash my face and eyes with water. After that, I barely could see anything out of the left-eye. Needless to say, I continued with the "Police Exam". From that moment on, my left-eye became very sensitive to light. If it were not for his laying of the hands on my eyes, who is to say which way my sight would have gone?

THE SKEPTIC

Dated: January 11, 2012 – Turned Believer

My second encountered with others having that capabilities, was when I went to the Ferndcliff X-Ray Medical Facility on January 5, 2012 to have my right hip X-rayed. By far I am the greatest skeptic, who have heard about people with the Healing Power called the "Laying On Of Hand" and never believed it possible. Well, I would never forget this one doctor that saw me and treated my hip problem. First, he took full X-rays of my body length to check for the cause of my excruciating pain of my right hip that felt like pinprick needles stabbing at it. After the X-rays of my full body length, he then lay his hand on my right hipbone and instantly I did not feel anything at all. That painful electricity and strange-ill sensation moving along my right hip was totally gone and I could now stand straight on both legs. Prior to that, I was putting all my weight to one side and leaning on one leg, and since then, I could do exercise without any pain. As skeptical as I was, I don't know if I would classify it as a miracle but by Thursday, January 12, 2012 I was totally cured. That man who did the X-ray had an aura of calmness and sort of a strange vibe.

CHAPTER XIX
THE ACCOMPLISHMENTS

Thinking Accomplishments Were Only Through Acquisition, Life Thought Me A Valuable Lesson In What Is Most Important?

What I have accomplished is my life back? The very substance of me. It is so easy to lose one sight of what really matters in life when accomplishment is equate to monetary values. Truth be told, monetary is dispensable while morality is infinite. Do not take my word for it, it is in the **"Bible".** Why did **GOD** give up **HIS** only begotten **SON** to save us, because there was one who was **"Just"?**

Funny thing is, you can go through life thinking you have it all and never be satisfied. Why is that? Because at some point in life, the focus got shifted from all about **"You"** to what life is really about? The ego part of us, always want to stand out and be noticed. Therefore, people acquired as much as they can in a lifetime. And even though, they have all the luxury, still they remain miserable, if not as miserable. Realizing that when they die, it cannot be taken with them.

In GOD'S world, the principle of sharing is strongly conveyed. Happiness is found through sharing. Life does not exist in one entity although, it is singular, it is comprised of many elements. To better understand life, is to accept JESUS into your life. The line that saved me was when I did just that, accept "JESUS".

After delving so deep into the **Abyss**, I did not know whether I was "coming" or "going"? Prayers kept me going. At times I was just going through the motion. I became desensitized to my surroundings. Nothing registered and nothing stayed! I was literally a blankslate walking. I had to relearn everything. It was weird because in my head, I knew the materials, but I just cannot make it stay. It was like an outer-self of me navigating through this crazy maze were my thoughts and words are being thrown back at me. It took a lot of willpower that kept me from going insane. So, I did what I knew best to do, started reading books. I have learned that my mind does not wonder when I would read books. I stayed focused and by the Grace of GOD, I was able to retain the information. So, I started going back to the libraries picking up books to read for about three to six years. After-a-while, when I felt that my mind was cleared up enough and I had retrained my mind to concentrate, I then decided to retake that darn "Exam" in year 2010 that had eluded me in year 2001 for so long. It is my nature! I like to finish what I started.

In October of 2010 I was able to pass that elusive "Exam" and by 2012 I completed the program and got my designation.

1. In 2011 I became Licensed Health Agent.
2. Then in 2012 I acquired my Life License.
3. In 2015 I am fully a Certified Home Health Aide.
4. By 2018 I am Licensed Securities Agent.

Nice Accomplishments! But it is pale to the gravitate of Dire Quotidian when she was Dire Quotidian for, she will never be hundred percent Dire Quotidian that she was. I have come to terms with it now and I lived my life being the best me.

Often at times, I do wish I could go back to being me, when I would get a glimpsed of the real Dire Quotidian looking back at me, but then again, a Christian of Faith should always remember the CRUCIFIX / PASSION OF CHRIST.

My Life's Reward: I got to live to accomplish my life coming back to me in full circle.

CHAPTER XX
THANKFULL

Being Thankful Is Easy When It Is The Reciprocal Of An Appreciation For What Someone Did For You. I, on the other hand, am grateful to my Families, my Catholic Church, the Monsignor, the Priests, the Friends and the many people I have encountered along the way wishing me well through prayers. Last but, not least, I am thankful for the littlest of the little ones who put a smile on my face during the Saturday's Religious Program.

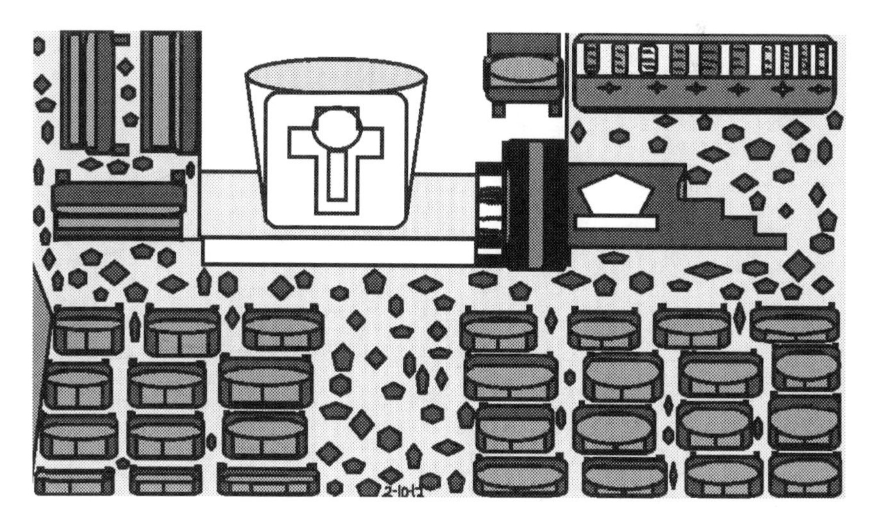

Figure 6

THANK YOU GOD FOR MY BEING

I was born in a Blackman's Land.
But I grew up in a Whiteman' Land.
Somewhere across the sea,
I must have lost my Sense of Being,
For I don't know whether I'm coming or going.

Some might say, I'm just Homesick,
But, how can I be Homesick?
When I don't even know where Home is at.
O! Feels like I'm living in a Noman's Land.

I've been on a Quest for so long,
Trying to find myself.
Always questioning of my Existence.
O! Feels like I'm losing my mind.

And just when I thought the end is near,
GOD whispered in my ear:
"My child, my child, my precious child,
I love you and I'm always with you."
And O! how my LORD,
"Grant me the serenity to accept
The things I cannot change,
The courage to change the things I can,
And the wisdom to know the Difference."
And now I know, and now I know with GOD,
I definitely have a place
To lay my weary head,
And to call my home.
For I am a somebody in my LORD'S eyes.
Thank you, GOD for my Being.

CHAPTER XXI

THE VIRTUE OF A PERSON'S IDENTITY

The Answer Is In Me. Sometimes when you looked for the truth elsewhere, you might come to the realization that it was always looking right back at you, if and only if, you took the time to notice and accept it for what it really is. **"It is what it is?"**

THE ANSWER

Often at times, we ask **why**?
Why this happen, why that happen?
Give no heed to **what**.
What cause of action taken for **why** to happen?
Then pondering at **when**.
When was it that **what** happen?
And try to place yourself at **where**.
Where were you or should you have been there?
But the questions keep adding up,
And the answers are few in coming.
Until you can answer the **who**?
That is when all the pieces will fit together,
And the answer within you will be unlocked.

Little did I know it then that throughout my tumultuous years, I needed not go far for the **answers** because they were always within me and my "**faith**". Time tested and it has been proven throughout ancient biblical history that the driven force to one's innate survival always stemmed from one's **"Faith". Because without "Faith", where does the soul seek "Answers"?** At the same token, I have come to understand why some people tend to lose their ways in crisis and stop looking for the answers within and instead rely on outside substances to alleviate the pain.

One thing for sure, not every pain is the same nor not everyone feels the same pain. **AMEN!!!**

Common mistake people tend to make is to prevent someone from relieving their pain. Grieving is the benefactor of pain. Then and only then does that come to pass.

My **"Why's?"** came from September 11, 2001. It was like stepping outside of my body and looking at the world through different lenses. Nothing made any sense and the impenetrable U.S.A. we all knew became vulnerable. New York State was at a standstill. I became a **"pariah".**

Instantly I became a target, a marked person and an outcast. I was no longer the Dire Quotidian that turned everything she touches into "gold" but someone to loath at. A lost identity with no direction but, the "Devil" walking among them. This was a strong burden to live with since I too was a citizen of the U.S.A. and I too, was also affected by this dreadful **"terrorist attack"** on the American Soil. Well needless to say, I was deemed the "Devil" and many people wished for my "demise". I kept going over and over around in my head. What did I do? What did I do? Only but for taking that damn "Exam". The minute that September 11 happened, I just knew right then and there that it was tied to that damn "Exam" I had just taken the day before. The data manipulation/the computer switch/and the fifteen (15) minutes off during the "Exam" all came rushing back to me.

(You tell me how one can come from that bottomless pit knowing and having the knowledge that you were intertwined in a sadistic manmade evil plot? My "Faith" kept me alive!)

My Answer Is: To quote from a Righteous Book, **the "Bible"; "Walk by Faith and not by Sight!"** Well, if they do not get it, then look them strict in the eyes next time they call you the "Devil" and say to them "Why? Because I lived?" For, you cannot imagine what kind of agenda they had plotted for your demise, only the **LORD** knows.

THE CREATOR already paved the steppingstone for your path in this borrowed time on Earth. Hence, when we tried to rush the hands of time and to go our own different ways, do not be surprised of all the **encounters** you have come to meet along the path for they too are lost souls going astray. The only way to stay in **righteousness** is to follow **GOD'S** plan for you.

CHAPTER XXII
FEELING LESS THAN A PENNY

Dated: 3/9/11 – If Ever In Your Lifetime Someone Makes You Feel Less Than A Penny?

When you have nothing but time in your hands, a true reflection of where you are and what have you become cannot escape the mind as I was reduced down to a penny on March 9, 2011 when I was sent to work in the State Parks Department?

PICK IT UP!
If ever in your lifetime,
Someone makes you feel less than a penny!
What do you do?
Pick It Up! Pick It Up! Pick It Up!

Find a penny, pick it up!
It's a way to Heaven up.

Five times the "Penny",
Trickle down the "Nickel",
Multiply by the "Franklin Dime",
Add in the "Quarter" twice,
Hallelujah to my LORD, thrice.
Get me to the "Hundredfold".
By Picking It Up! Pick It Up! Pick It Up!

True, it did take 30 COINS
To betray the trust of a "Good Friend".
Howbeit then, that a "Penny" can keep you down?
When JESUS made it to HIS Destination,
By Picking It Up! Pick It Up! Pick It Up!
Hence, if ever you are looking
For example, to pick it up?
Remembered how JESUS
Travelled the path to the Cross.
No, it wasn't easy?
No, it wasn't smooth?
Neither was it painless?
Despite the fall three times,
He Picked It Up! Pick It Up! Pick It Up!

Find a "Penny", pick it up!
It's a way to Heaven up.

Therefore, if someone can
Make you feel less than a "Penny",
It is because you relinquished
Your power over to them.
Never give up your power,
But do Pick It Up! Pick It Up!
That's the only way to Heaven up.

If memories served me well, at this point in time, I really can't remember what transpired to have me worked in the State Parks Department? But one thing for sure, it was done out of malice. Regardless of the malicious intentions at that moment in time, nevertheless, I would not take away from the experiences of working there as it thought me a valuable lesson and gave me insight to real lives' lessons where people are made to feel less than a "penny". The journey I travelled picking it up, day in and day out would have crumbled a lesser spirit. But in my mind's eyes, I was rebuilding myself and using the opportunity to never forgot those who helped me pick it up along my darkest paths. In all, I spent a total of six months there. By three years later, when my braincells started to replenish and formulate some sense of it all that looking back I fully grasped the gravitate of it all that this was no accident at all, but instead a well-orchestrated move to have me get lost in the criminal system. Therefore, this is not about me, but about the overall big picture. It must have been GOD'S sent that I got out of the job in the nick of time for I did not come out of it unscathed. I had a big target on my back, and I got a big bumped bruised on my forehead by the garbage truck's back pulley as I went to dump the garbage in. (Wow!!! What a nightmare it would have been indeed, to have gotten pulled inside the truck along with the garbages?) I am not a **"superwoman"** but that experienced surely made me feel like a **"superwoman"!**

CHAPTER XXIII
KEEPING THE FAITH

Life Can Be Very Testing, Thus Constantly Trying One's Faith. Like the Old Adage says, "If it is not broken, why fix it?" With much do respect to the beginning of the introduction page, where it posed the question, "Do you believe in God'? Please do not try to curtail your answer so as to please the questioner but do so because your "faith" is as strong as your "belief". Simply just say **"YES, I BELIEVE IN GOD",** no more and no less**.**

When people do dance around the question like life throws them a curve it can get increasingly difficult to answer while it becomes harder to maneuver a right or wrong answer by staying true to themselves? With all its "ups" and "downs", its "twists" and "turns", its "chaos" and "destructions", how can one not keep the **"Faith"** in all this? Believe me, trust in GOD. Remember that HE is, the **"Alpha"** and the **"Omega"**.

Yes! Life can be very demanding, someday you will come to the realization that it is when your faith remains steadfast in its conviction, that your problems will be resolved. And when you shall look back on it one day, it is then you would realize that it was a life's lesson needed to be learned? Do you not know that life is a constant yet unpredictable which makes it that much interesting to live?

CHAPTER XXIV
LIFE REWARD

A Miracle Of Prayer: Through Hard Work And Determination, Comes Self-proclamation.

July 28, 2008

LIGHTED CANDLE

The lighted candle's flame shoots upright,
As if in keeping pace with each prayer.
Does it really speak?
Or is it the flame interacting with the air?

Who is to say?
But the lighted candle,
That speaks many verses in its luminous radiance.

With each sharp projectile flame rises,
It is answering prayers time and time again.
When each flame majestically rises to the
Point of elevation,
Then the spirits are speaking.

The lighted candle like in the Gospels,
Represents the LIGHT within that cannot be distinguished.

My Life Reward: Is knowing that I came from hell and back without distinguishing my light and keeping it shining. As long, as I believed that GOD was with me, I had the power to turn my light on and off. **GOD IS LIGHT! AMEN!!!**

CHAPTER XXV

THE SCAPEGOAT

Dated: May 19, 2006

To Discredit A Person, Is To Make That Person Seems Unbelievable?

But one thing with me, is that, they did not count on my exactness for details and keen sense of reality. My organizational skills, stickler for details, and insightfulness.

1) My Haiti Vacation Pictures ----Four(4) Roll of Films that came back blank and empty at the Squarespace Photo Shop (back then KODAK was in existence).
2) My "Exam1" Test Scores------Questionable?
3) The "Exam" Test Score-------With the two computers switch; 15 minutes into the Exam.
4) The Auto Incident Of 7/99-----After coming out of the Furniture Store on Quelchetown Avenue in County Banque.
5) The Screw In The Backtire------Where the "baby" was sleeping in her carseat?
6) The Almost Heart-Attack-------After seeing that smashed rat/mouse by my car in the parking lot at the job.
7) That Little Boy-------Who broke the flower vase at Adleine's daughter birthday party where I brought her the doll for present?

8) My Watch That Was Stolen------On the platform of the subway on route to "The City" Interview on Thursday, April 5, 2001. **(My beautiful Rubies and Diamonds Ring)**

9) The Mishap With The Wicker Chair------As I purchased one for my niece's welcoming to the world.

10) The Broken Head Of The Virgin Mary's Statue-----That was on my desk.

11) The Big Bloody Mess------In the bathroom that woman **Clavice Bruns** pointed out to me as I walked in from my lunch hour at 12pm to 1pm.

[???I still think that there was a real baby on the floor. A premature baby→ whether it survived it is anybody guessed.]

12) The Coffee Stain On The Brand New Carpet------Running down the hallway along the kitchen entrance. (Someone may have done this on purpose for there was a saying that was going around that "the big boss is a real sticker for cleanliness"

[*I could never understand why they dropped that coffee on the carpet in the hallway by the kitchen?*]

What A Character? A Character Is Knowing Who You Are And What You Are?

Sometimes in life, you must become a character in order to combat whatever mishaps that come your way so as not to fall prey to victimization. It does not necessary mean to be arrogant or obnoxious? Instead, is to humble oneself and become meek and humble like JESUS**, the Victorious One.**

Dated: June 28, 2007

The "Infamous" $2,000.00 duplications retrieved from the TAEPNA Account Plan, is finally coming to light for me. I just stumbled upon a receipt from the medical place that I had visited on August 26, 1999 due to a minor incident at the workplace where I had bumped my right arm against the cubicle's partition and my right wrist swelled up badly on that day. Therefore, the supervisor suggested that I go seek treatment for it immediately and hence, I left the job that day with permission to get treatment.

That is right off the County Central Parkway, close by the State University. I paid in cash the $15.00 co-pay. In any event, this would have been no big deal except for some strange reason, TAEPNA always sent me a statement detailing the charges and treatments received from the doctors but in this particular event not a statement was sent to me. Although, I had requested it from them numerous times, I still had no success in receiving one. What is striking about the whole thing, again, is going back to the dates in question?

That date of visit 8/26/99 is closely related to the beginning of the month where upon one worker pointed out to me a bloody situation on the company's bathroom floor on (8/2/99????). And it also closely related to the duplication of my TAEPNA's Account for a $2,000.00 withdrawal signed off on September 21, 1999. Something really strange was going on and since then, I always felt creepy that someone was always watching me. How creepy is that to be always watched by an unknown and not knowing where you stand with that person?

JULY 6, 2007

Today in church, this woman approached me after mass by the bookshelves. She struck up a conversation with me as if she knew me from the past and for the life of me, I was trying to remember her but could not.

Later, her features kind of reminded me of this Jamaican woman I used to know Adleine St. Charles (the woman whose house I stayed in preparing for the "Exam2" in year 1999). The thing that is disturbing about the whole situation is that for some unknown reason, the car incident on Quelchetown Avenue and being stopped by the cop for ten (10) minutes on the Turnpike to take my license information started to conjure up some strange memories that are bizarre and made no sense to me at all.

Noteworthy is that, anyone can run a Department of Motor Vehicle on an individual and get more personal and specific information than a non-insurance adjuster. Why would someone like her wanted to get information on me? It is up for grabs unless as my instincts were telling me, this whole thing could have led to what now have become suspicious activities to my identity as misappropriation. Many reasons, firstly, she was aware about my upcoming "Exam2" in the first week of January 1999. I needed some quiet time a sanctuary place to really get some study done and as a friend she welcomed me into her house, and I stayed there about a week and one day before the exam in January. During that time, I was already sick with the flu (fever, rash, and diarrhea) as I had previously mentioned before in **Chapter 3 Page 18** and when I came to her house, I was recovering from the flu. I was determined to take the "Exam2" and so I forged ahead anyway. Secondly, sometimes in March 1999, Adleine, her girlfriend and I went to MAZES, in her black Toyota Jeep and out of gratitude on my part, since she allowed me to stay at her house, I bought them both some sweaters with my credit card. Now this business about the sweater is the fact that at the office Christmas gift-exchange in December, this Mr. Owen gave me a box containing a man's gray pullover sweater. Thirdly, is the jeep being a brand of Toyota, for all the time I have known her, I was the one with the Toyota Tercel and she had a small brown minivan. The woman friend came that one night and I never saw her again. Why this descriptive narration of the Toyota is that, on my credit report, I have this address attached to my name doing business as Transportation Service? In any event, I count my blessings that I had stayed a week there and not the two full weeks originally planned. What was the purpose of staying longer there when I had already taken the test and plus, her husband and small daughter at the time were away on vacation, she could always call that girlfriend of hers? Truth be told, I did not feel comfortable staying there anymore, I was sick as a dog and wanted the comfort of my home. Although, I will always be thankful to her for making some remedies that made me felt much better. Better enough to go on and took that darn "Exam2".

Now this business about the Caliber Zone cruise to Barrnone Line from Pochmarck from sales-representatives Adleine/Heather sounded too fishy for me, since I had already been on a cruise in May 1999. This was going back to the proximate location of where Adleine's wedding took place at the church and the reception at the catering hall afterwards. I was invited, and I attended both. And for that occasion, I had the opportunity to wear my "green dress" with my white handbag and wearing my beautiful **gold**

Seiko watch with the beautiful **rubies/diamonds ring.** In retrospect, for some mysteriously reason and years later both the watch and the ring happened to go missing in a subway incident traveling to "Central City". I have come to believe that I was lured into a phony job interview for that purpose. It was also there, that I have met Adleine's sister Chezraine who was with her fiancé for the first time. You know when you have that feeling that you don't belong there, well, that was the impression her sister Chezraine gave me. In any event, I never received a copy of the pictures they took, although I had asked for a copy. We have lost communication with time. And life was moving really fast for the both of us. Fast forward to year 2001, we probably all went through hell trying to make sense of **"What The Hell Is Happening In America?"**

Looking back, I am thinking when the last time I had gone to Adleine's house was sometime after the car incident in later part of July or August. But being so frazzled and distracted, I could not asked her the right questions on cases of automobile incidents as she was an adjuster and I needed her expertise on the matter especially, now that time have passed. But she was dismissive, something about her demeanor was different and her inattentiveness to her little daughter needed to be changed from her soiled diapers while inside the garage, should have told me to back off. Now is not the time. Well, I kept thinking to myself, when is she going to change the diapers? Needless to say, I too was not at all smelling great myself. I was reeking with the smell of sewage (maybe it was her way of saying to me at that time I stunk). I did and did not know it at that time. I reeked with the smell of sewage.

CHAPTER XXVI

TOTAL DESTRUCTION! THE DAY HAITI STOOD STILL!

January 12, 2010 – Monday

Words Sometime Can Be A Prediction! Little did I knew it then what I know now about writing of my missing pictures vacationing in my Country, Haiti of my birthplace in year 1997 would have come to a rectifying consequence in years later to come? For the second time, in year 2007 I made another visit to my birthplace, Haiti. And then, in year 2010 that uneventful 7.0 Major Earthquake hitting Haiti and completely destroying the country, my heart sank. All Port-Au-Prince destroyed and under rubbles as miles and miles of concretes, bricks and stones collapsed that brought the Country, Haiti under total chaos. It was estimated about 300,000 were dead. Presidential Palace totally destroyed. Government, Parliament, Hospitals, Banks, and Schools, all destroyed.

That tremendous earthquake registering a magnitude of 7.0 opened Haiti up to its core. What a massive destruction? Sorry to say, don't mess with GOD'S child. Trying to make me think I was going crazy or better, yet she is her father's child. No, my father Mr. Quotidian was neither a lunatic nor insane, he just got caught up in his enemies' wrongdoings (started with jealousy for his great mind).

Haiti did not deserve what happen to it but then evils roamed among the innocence, hence as in any casualty, the innocence does suffer, and fatality is part of their very existence.

But Enough Is Enough, when too many innocences' blood have been shed. Afterall, Jesus did shed his blood for us on the cross so as not to have what happened, happened. The day of judgment is definitely insight and not too far in the distance.

This uneventful history in Haiti's past will forever be sketched in my memory. I can't seem to get away from it when still to this present day in time (2013) the country is partially rebuilt, repaired and restructured. **For heaven's sake, what will it take to get some common sense into the minds of those in power that it is not always about the monies but about servicing the peoples you claimed to have their best interests in mind?** What are the powers to be waiting for? Life moves in stages and that is forward, it cannot reverse itself but can only forge ahead with the span of time given therefore, what the heck is wrong with the mentalities of those so-called intellects of want-to-be "King Solomon". Wisdom is not something acquired along the way, either you have it or was born with it or you might just want to settle for being who you are (lack luster in the basic of human compassion). Those peoples have suffered long and hard and still are suffering. Common decency should prevail in such a matter so trite and so vast that time is truly of the essence. History is there to teach us not to repeat past errors and yet Haiti seems to be making the same mistakes time and time again.

CHAPTER XXVII

MAKESHIFT INVESTIGATION

When In A Bind Become Your Own Makeshift Sleuth? I started doing my own investigation. Back tracking my every step and keeping logs of pertinent events.

MAY 7, 2012

A Force To Reckon With, is a literature reading about a novel of a concept that entwines with true biography. It will captivate, enlighten, intrigue, mesmerize, and spellbound you. It is like walking on water without the fear of sinking.

HOW LIFE HAS A WAY OF COMING BACK IN FULL CIRCLE?

How idiots make carbon copies of me as if I was an object with no respect to someone's privacy, thinking that I would be impressed with their version of idiotic Baccawoods?

I have this "egnema" about me! I don't like the word cannot and no that is the one thing you do not say to me; for it acts like my catalyst to prompt me to surge to excellence at what I do.

There is a proverb that goes: Silence is deafening but “Words” are weapons.

I do not say much, but when I talk, I speak the “truth” and every square inch of the “truth” and give “insight” to whatever that does not want to be revealed.

CHAPTER XXVIII
THE WORST AND THE MOST HUMILIATING DAY

Dated: Wednesday, June 5, 2013 – The Subway Incident

It Felt Like The End Of The World To Me. As every morning started out like a routine, I got ready, drank my cup of coffee and a cup of water afterwards and then head out the door to take the bus at the bus stop. Everything went accordingly until I got to the Fortbound Stop, just one stop to where I got off on Waykrauss Street. My bladder could not hold it anymore, I saw this idiotic, imbecility man (black male) and beg him please, please, please to let me use the bathroom as I saw him with some chains of keys in his hand. He was accompanied by another man (white male) and he answered me "No!" because there was no bathroom on this platform and said to me that I could go right there on the corner to relieve myself. **The audacity of that man,** to tell me to go relieve myself on the platform for all eyes to see and coming trains on the tracks. Wow! Talked about pure stupidity, pure meanness, pure carelessness and pure insensitivity. Unimaginable that someone would say that to someone in need of emergency. I was doing the "peepee dance" for crying out loud. I told him no I would not do that and that is when he pointed to the stairs and told me that outside there is a restaurant I could go to. Hence, I went through the glass doors and up the stairs almost reaching the top to the street when it just came out, I mean right there, between the two levels of stairs heading up to the street. I just stood there and peep on myself. Boy-oh-Boy! All the while, I was slowly dying inside. But despite that meanness jerk, the commuters travelling to work on that un-fateful morning coming out of the Fortbound platform and witnessed to my non-glorious moment did not jeered, smirked or said anything. **Wow, something to be said about Americans that they are decent people. Someone even took pity on me and took the time to try and helped me.** I will never live this one down. It would be a forever sketched memory in my brains and one thing for sure is that what goes in is unforgettable. My pants were soaking wet from totally drenched peep. I called my boss and told him I had an incident and would not be able to come to work that day. Needless to say; I found myself outside of Fortbound's platform, I had no choice but to come up and out onto the street, then crossed over to the other side to get back on to the opposite platform going the opposite way back home meanwhile I am soaking wet from peep. I got in the subway and in the trains heading back the opposite way home with a drenched wet pants and every commuter watching. How did I make it back home is still a mystery for it felt like this "Daymare" was going on forever? I mustered enough strength to go to work the next day, Thursday, June 6, 2013 and I had enough sense to take pictures of the area because I still can't believe that idiot told me to go right there. Then on Friday, June 7, 2013, at the same Fortbound Platform I saw two city plain clothes metro workmen, I approached them and asked, "How does one go about reporting an incident that took place here on this platform?" One gave me some cuckoo-bull story and the other acted like he did not understand.

I said it before that "**LIFE HAS A WAY OF COMING BACK IN FULL CIRCLE**" and it is true. Because I am always calling people "poopoo head" when they do something annoying, I now become a "peepee head".

Now, I should take my own advice and heed to my own warnings, for I became the opposite of what I used to call people, a "peepee head". See in my case, I actually peep on myself. Thanks in part to that "jerk".

***My Eyes have seen so many things,
And my Ears have heard too many things,

But my Mouth remains silence,
And now the Rocks are speaking untruths.
Things that are lies, lies, lies***

(****Does not this remind you of Chapter VII – "The Subway Incident" where it is Déjà vu all over again except different nightmare with different outcome****).

Really, I did not set out to write a story of my life but to keep accounts of events that nearly destroyed me and a way of also **"self-therapeutic"** to relieve me from stresses and toxics build-up of anger. But in the end, it turned out to be my punching bag.

CHAPTER XXIX
REVELATION

WHAT THE FIG???

Dated: August 18, 2013

Enough of their STUPIDITIES!!! They are so SWEET!!!

Knoorblart Clinic-----------Focused my RearEnd (Hypocritical Oath: First and foremost do no harm.)

Supermarket--------------Inappropriate (Why? Wanted the whole damn foodmarket for yourself.)

Church---------------------Crazy (Most Sanctified Event of the Church -Station of the Cross.)

Organization-------------Yelled at / Bathroom Encounter (Had to relieve myself/solo.)

Assembly--------------Lazy (Learns the facts before assuming.)

Home-----------------------Rude (Reciprocal: Give and Receive.)

They all have one thing in common that is they are all **females** of the upmost self-righteousness and the biggest **hypocrites of the faith**!!! Duplicity is Stupidity.

Last memory and last time I made to feel like curling up into a ball like a fetus and just give up. Now I am back and taking no "pity" and never again to second guess myself that is when I make **mistakes**.

Watch out and Beware I have been through "hell and back".

Tired of eating **ICE**!!!

Let out the **FIRE**!!!

Cont. of Revelation - August 24, 2013

Current Driver License Photo: This is what they are depicting as the "Monkey". Well, a Monkey Sees and a Monkey Does!

I don't have a problem with that remark other than the fact that I set the **precedent** for the "black and white fashion statement". Is not a "Monkey" sees and does therefore, why am I being copied, followed and my every words and logics stolen?

The Driver License Photo represents a trial in my life that unbeknownst to me have documented that "idiot" ill-wills toward me as a result of the residual effects from being "focused".

Then I came to light that they were checking for my "Adam's Apple", that is why my neck is extended that way because I was told to lift-up my head a little bit more each time before she took the darn picture. Why??? All it showed is that I have a long neck, my beauty mark.

And to top it all, I still don't look that bad even when I am at my worst condition. See I could take pictures without makeup can I say the same for you.

Now, let's take a step back into the revelation of time when I was sitting inside the classroom preparing for the "Exam2" when out of nowhere, that darn instructor made a sarcastic remark pertaining to someone being **"ugly"**, and if you were born **"ugly"**, you will always be **"ugly"**, no matter the cosmetic surgery.

Well, I am not here to play guessing games nor peek-a-boo, but I am **"naturelle"**. I am just tired of everytime I go somewhere to have someone following, screaming, yelling and commenting at "moi". What the Fig??? I do not recall having a Paparazzi. But this is getting to be annoying and unnerving. Hence my driver license speaks for itself!!!

Hence, the driver license picture is tied to the **deliberately targeted car incident on July 18, 1999** on Quelchetown Avenue. Of Course, the Department Of Motor Vehicle is right on top of the 103rd Police Precinct. I always felt it was much more than that, but I could never pinpoint anything when you only have pieces and pieces and pieces of information. **Kaleidoscope of Information.** When memories collided with facts, that is when all the pieces come nicely together?

THE COMMON DENOMINATOR

For Things To Equal, must find what is common between them even if the Numerator may vary, but the Denominator **must** always be the same.

NUMERATOR:

1) Time; Day; Images; People
2) Places visit
3) At the Job - I told Supervisor and Workers
4) People I used to be close to→
5) Midnight Rainy Wedding→

DENOMINATOR: Cannot be me, because I am doing the action, I am taking the pictures. passport was not in my possession then for my uncle said he would hold onto it for safe keeping. Still pondering about my "passport" not being in my possession and may have been compromised???

*** CAMERA
*** Four(4) Rolls Of films
*** 1997 – Two (2) weeks of vacation to relax and refamiliarize myself with my birth country.
*** Profoundly affected by the situations over there (No Improvement).
*** It changed my life. I wanted and needed to help→as if something transformed me; like a calling that I can make a difference.

CHAPTER XXX
KALEIDOSCOPE

When Memories Collided With Facts?

Life is a series of stages moving along in an endless twist of events. As in a reverse reflection of an image from a mirror, a new life evolved as memories that were once submerged into the abyss of Kaleidoscope surface, hence life is restored. Fragmented pieces of events coming together like pieces of puzzle to form a whole as stored information from the subconscious is brought at will to the conscience recalling facts. Just like stages in life, I went from **Awareness**, to **Questions**, then **Answers**, to **Closure**, and finally **Acceptance**. Therefore, memory is the embodiment of life experiences that measure self-worth and wisdom. Notwithstanding, if memory is lacking then intelligence is nonexistence and the ability to resolve difficult questions remains dogma.

I used to be keen, sharp and a stickler for details but lately I have been confused. I seemed to repeat things over and over when I should have gotten them from the start. This process requires a lot of energy and I have exerted too much energy just to keep it level and not go off on a tangent. I relied on my strength to keep me going whenever I felt like I am slowing down. I can't seem to get simple things into perspective, and it scared me. I have always measured my life-worth by my intelligence and therefore, since I have been experiencing difficulties at recalling information at will, I get frustrated, annoyed and agitated. I don't like what was happening and I don't understand why it was happening. Because this is not me, the person that I am is sharp and wise. Through it all, I tried not to prejudge anything said nor revealed until I get all the facts and not to jump to any conclusion. By the grace of GOD and my faith, I will jot down whatever glimpse of memories that come to mind. I am glad that I did because they will serve as details of factual occurrences of the truth. And now all my questions will be answered as my memories are revealed overtime. No longer would I count on outside influences to answer my questions for the answers are within me, safely locked in my memories. I prayed and prayed GOD for my memories and for his help and HE has answered my prayers.

STAGE I - PUTTING THE PIECES TOGETHER

Lately, I'm having my memories back again, I feel like me, strong, confident and positive. Now, I need not bother people anymore with so many questions that they cannot answer for me. What am I missing? Why cannot I put the pieces together? Little did I know that each time, I was turning my light off and each time **GOD** turns it back on. **GOD** fortifies my strength and gives me courage to seek the truth. The truth is the **Kaleidoscope** of memories that cannot be disputed by others' lies and untruths. Now I understand why I had difficulties remembering because I suppressed due to shock and that incident with the car created by that person/persons in the blueish car and the white car, and as a result, I suffered mental distress as well as physical distress. **I am me again;** and can face my adversaries with newfound confidence. As long as GOD is with me noone can harm me. I am not afraid of their terror nor what manner of evil sayings they say about me. I have the courage to change things and the power to take back my life. And with this newfound **"answers"** to enlightenment, I was beginning to put all the pieces together. And now I know why the events of the smashed dead mousse by the car in the parking lot, and the day the kids were in my car when the child car seat was installed exactly on the same side, and the snowy day when the car battery was borrowed and the loud cursing music playing behind my parked car in the driveway by the other car. Leaning evermore on my **"faith"** that is endless, after one's been put through trials and errors, the only thing that is left is the **"Truth"**. Consequently, how does one bring faith into the **Kaleidoscope** of life?

Today, I woke up (8/11/03) with vivid remembrance of things: I felt awful because I was responsible for the kids being in my car but I put myself through when I should not have because it was Grinch who put the children in the seats in the back of the car in the parking lot and it is him who also put that thing through the back rear tire for who none other than Grinch waiting for me when I got back to the house with the kids as if he had already known something. And why did not I get it before, it was him who quickly took the kids out and took the car to get the tire changed without even letting me pay for it. He paid for the work! My Goodness, why did not I remember this before? It is both Grinch and Karmar who plotted this sabotage also, it is Karmar who took the battery out of the car. Now going back to the Koorblart thing, again it was none other than Karmar waiting for me on the balcony. Why did not I see all this before? They set me up at my job and sabotage my job. On Quelchetown Avenue, the car incident was staged by them that's what that guy was trying to tell me when he wrote that name down. He tried to warm me and hinted at it, but I just could not get it. The name and the car should have given me a clue. On the sales there was the name. Now, I have the power to do something about this all.

STAGE II - SANITY KEEPSAKE

Dated: August 30, 2007

There Must Have Been Something In The Water. When things that were there before seemed to disappear? When you know for sure it is not your sanity that is going, but mere case of deception? How creepy to know that it was your mind that they were going after. Wow!!! You proved them wrong that you were not easily erasable? Although, they played their games for your piece of mind. Truth can be told that a picture is worth a thousand words. Many pictures covered the wall of doomed, leading to the Bloody Mess in the Bathroom, but it was the screw in the tire that sets you **ablaze**. When a quiet, humble and reserve person is deemed gullible, just remembered how the Great Walls of Jericho came tumbling down with the power of simple prayers? And for Sanity Keepsake, this would be your TESTAMENT of reality.

CHAPTER XXXI
MY WAKE UP CALL!

YEAR 2015 - (From August 2015 to March 2018)

After going through yet another rollercoaster of trying to find a job, I landed in a new venture with the health fields as Home Health Aide. Little did I know it then, it turned out to be a "Blessings In Disguise". What I have learned and would always take with me is immensely? The jobs started out as any other jobs and so I thought, but I got a priceless education and a vast array of knowledge. Normally, I am used to a stationary position inside an Office Building, but this venture took me on many different journeys where I can but get out of my comfort zone. Even as I am writing this text the memories floating back like tidal waves. Because everyone of my clients that I had the opportunity to meet with, they have left me with a profound understanding of humanity and valuable lessons that would impacted my life forever. Although the circumstances of which I came into their lives were sad, needless to say, I enjoyed some and would miss most. I got to hear and be fascinated with their stories, insights, life experiences and histories that were priceless. As in a good thing, the one downside to it was the short-lived moments I got to spend with them. As a person who relished in my own solitude, I really enjoyed spending quality time with most of them as they were an asset to my development and human preservation. There is indeed a purpose to life, even when you don't see it right away, something magical would happen that makes you get out of your own way and force you to reality. And that is exactly what happened to me? Having this Home Health Aide job at that moment in time was no coincidental for time is relevant and things happen according to its timing.

During the two years and nine months working as Home Health Aide, I did not have time to ponder and say, "Why Me?" anymore. Life forces you to realize that regardless you participate in it or not, it continues with or without you.

Lessons well learned and well deserving just in time. Kudos to all the tireless Home Health Aides! I know sometimes it may not feel that you Aides are "valued", and you are made to feel that you are part of the **"Deplorable Workers"** but GOD sees it differently as you are providing an irrecompensable services that is restoring Human Dignity back to the clients. **I know, I walked the walk!**

Keep in mind when they sniffed at you or commented on your bodily order from a long day of work, just pictured (**soap, bottle of water and towel/ napkins**) for stanch could always be washed away, while STUPIDITY is INBORN and can never be washed away. There is nothing that can be done about it.

RESIDUAL EFFECT

Dated: May 7, 2019

Always and forevermore, I shall carry this residual effect inside of me that creeps up when least expected. As for being one hundred (100) percent recovery, it would never be in my case, for I am predestined to shortness-of-breath, tangling-of-the-fingers, memory-lapse, disorientation, and off-balance.

'Till this day, it is still a daily struggle for me to do anything. And to think that those "bozos" would not give me any disability compensation?

CHAPTER XXXII
SHOULD HAVE BEEN MY FULL CIRCLE?

Year: 2018

Today is December 23, 2018, two days before Christmas! I have gone through many "Ups" and "Downs" throughout the year but then, it proved to be very rewarding for I have obtained my Securities License and embarked on a new Career Endeavors with yet again another new company in the Financial Industries. As for my "Full Circle", eventually I would get there, but I sense the hesitation is with my unfulfilled purpose. **What is that Purpose?** Finished what I had started, the damn book, "THIS BOOK".

REALIZATION: I have come to accept and to realize that the possibility of the combination of the 1998 "flu shot" and the September 1999 Knoorblart's Office might have contributed to my health drastically deteriorated and my mind affected from intentional negligence. I don't know what was in that flu shot nor what was in the water from the colonoscopy but one thing for sure, I nearly died.

LIFE MATTERS!

Have you ever come across a lake where,
The water is still and perfectly intact?
Then you throw a rock and it makes ripples and waves.

Well, life is like a standing water,
still and motionless.
Until you go out there and start experiencing things
Making ripples and waves along the way,
Nothing happens.
Afterall, life is a statement that says,
"I am not just about being but also I am about LIVING."

CHAPTER XXXIII
REVOLUTION TO RESOLUTION

Started With A Dream; Ended With A Self-Assessment. Sometimes dreams alone are not guaranteed without some compromises along the way. Amen to that! Having an enlightenment did not come easy or fast but rather as a turtle pacing and sprinting to the finish line?

"Voices of Reason" can at times be an impediment if, but only if, one is not willing to admit to the **"Truth". What is then the Truth? The "Truth" at times, can be based on the prism at which one is looking through the lenses and although there is no right or wrong way, still, one is not immune to mistakes.** It is through **mistakes** in life that one has truly experienced the passages of life.

Throughout my many **"Ups" and "Downs",** I have heard a lot of uninvited **schmucks,** listened to a lot of unsolicited **advices** and pretended to benefit from some wisdom when reality is screaming at me the fundamentals; that no two lives, regardless of the similarities in experiences turn out the same. Parallels are relatable but never intertwined therefore given the same situation, one person might experience it positively while the other person experience it negatively. Until it can be explained where Parallel meets in the realm of time, then for now, welcome into my WORLD.

Once I had that eye-opener through enlightenment, it is then, I have decided that I am taking control back of my life.

RESOLUTION tend to have the connotation of resigning to a lesser you than where you were. But I beg to differ and say that, noone can live each other's experiences and noone can predict the outcome. Hence, I keep going back to "The Virtue Of A Person's Identity."

THE VIRTUE OF A PERSON'S IDENTITY

DIRE, if someone had told you
There would come a time in your life,
Where you would be recycled, reused, repaired
You would not have believed it?
Could it then be a test of your strength, your character?
For what does not break you, makes you strong.
True! But there is a limit to what a person can take.
Being passive does not mean it is a sign of weakness
Contrary it is a sign of restrain,
Because too much force needs a **balance.**

But what if someone had told you
After all that have passed,
You would be refreshed, rejuvenated, renewed
Would you have believed it then?
Maybe! But life is not about predictions.
It is about one's innate will to survive.
It is about one's ability to withstand life's many challenges
And the true test of one's identity.
For my life has been strengthen **8X** by a fortuitous
Force that has compelled me to **survive.**

CHAPTER XXXIV
COMING TO A FULL CIRCLE

Hence "A Force To Reckon With" Comes Back In Full Circle To Life! Having gone through what I went through and making it to the other side is nothing short of a "miracle"? It definitely changes you and your perception of life. You are not the same and you will never **be** the same. Somehow, I came back with a Six Sense and Insights beyond my understanding as well as more sensitivity to outside's **influences and stupidities**. I have become immune from "False Prophets" of modern time claiming to have insight into **Revelation** when it makes it absolutely clear not to **add** nor **remove** anything from its **writings.**

Hence, I have Come To A Full Circle By Learning To Let Go Of The Past And Crossing The Bridge.

CROSSING THE BRIDGE

Walking the distance is no bother, my feet go where the path Leads.
As I came to the bridge and stood there for awhile,
contemplating whether to cross the bridge or turned back to hence I came from.
→A little voice whispered, "Should I cross the Bridge?"
Looking far ahead, I do not know what awaits, but where I came, that I am certain.

A quick glanced of my surroundings, told me that everything looked fine.
In that instant, I felt my body moving forward across the bridge,
And each step I took, led me closer to the other side.
But in the middle of the bridge, and half-way to and from panic set in,
As the clouds hovered above about me and the waters pounced below at my feet.
→That little voice whispered again, "Should I cross the Bridge?"

Knowing I cannot go on and frozen in motion, I decided to wait it out 'til tomorrow.
Standing there felt like an eternity as the clouds condensed and the waters surged on.
Closing my eyes, I could hear the echoing of the waves clasping together at my rightside,

Then at my leftside and below me.
Opening my eyes again, I saw nothing but the darkness of the clouds.
At that moment, I felt tears running down my cheeks as I crouched down and prayed it pass.

But my tears were of no consolation, they only added to the waters about me and making
the waves that more relentless.
The night went on vengefully and tomorrow came yet still no change.
What to do? Did not matter anymore?
→Again, that little voice whispered, "Should I cross the Bridge?"

I stood up and looked toward Heavens above (in my mind's eyes) piercing the condensed clouds, I asked the Heavenly Father,
"**Lord** did I come this far to perish by the wayside why haven't you helped me?" No response.
I asked the **Lord** again for some intervention and yet, no response.
At that moment, I felt helpless as I let everything out bawling like a baby, quivering, ranting and shaking and all.
It was then My Heavenly Father said to me, "Of ye little faith that I can command the sea and the sky."

"Was not I who told Peter to walk on the water in the middle of a raging storm toward me?

And was it not when Peter took his eyes off me that he fell in the water? Then why must you, my child doubt, even as a baby, you first learned to crawl then to walk, fall then pick yourself up and walk again?"

"Howbeit, you searched for me in the Heavens and believed I exist even when you see me not?"

"Have I not guided your way?" "When you first set out on the path to crossing the Bridge in My Name, I was with you then and I am with you now?"

That is when, the Heavens cleared up and the waters subsided, my path became known to me from where I came and to where I am going.

→At last, the little voice whispered to me that, "Crossing the Bridge is to let go of the past and moving forward."

[I am not claiming to have all the "ANSWERS", but I am claiming that I know what I know from what I have gone through and from what was revealed to me.]

THE VIRTUE OF A PERSON'S IDENTITY

Printed in the United States
by Baker & Taylor Publisher Services